# BABY ROOMS

# BABY ROOMS

**Creating the Perfect Space for Your Baby to Grow In**

**by Warren Shoulberg**

**HPBooks**
a division of
PRICE STERN SLOAN
Los Angeles

**A FRIEDMAN GROUP BOOK**

Copyright © 1989 by Michael Friedman Publishing Group, Inc.

Published by HP Books,
a division of
Price Stern Sloan, Inc.,
360 North La Cienega Boulevard
Los Angeles, California 90048

**Library of Congress Cataloging-in-Publication Data**

Shoulberg, Warren.
    Baby rooms / by Warren Shoulberg.
        p.      cm.
    Includes index.
    ISBN 0-89586-736-2 : $24.95 ($32.95 Can.).     ISBN 0-89586-737-0
(pbk.) : $9.95 ($12.95 Can.)
    1. Interior decoration.      2. Nurseries—Equipment and supplies.
3. Nurseries—Safety measures.      I. Title.
NK2117.N87S56 1989
747.7'7—dc19                                                        88-12125
                                                                          CIP

*BABY ROOMS: Creating the Perfect Space for Your Baby to Grow In*
was prepared and produced by
Michael Friedman Publishing Group, Inc.
15 West 26th Street
New York, New York 10010

Editor: Sharon Kalman
Designer: Fran Waldmann
Art Director: Mary Moriarty
Photo Editor: Christopher Bain
Photo Researcher: Daniella Nilva
Production Manager: Karen Greenberg
Illustrations: Kenneth Spengler

Typeset by BPE Graphics, Inc.
Color separations by South Seas International Press Ltd.
Printed and bound in Hong Kong by Leefung-Asco Printers Ltd.

# Dedication

To Michele, who was there . . . and not there, as needed;
to Nancy, who remembered me; to Chelsea,
who kept the top of my Mac warm; and to David,
Todd, and Lauren, who have been fun (not to mention
educational) to watch grow up.

Courtesy Lamb's & Ivy

# CONTENTS

## Introduction

Page 8

# Introduction

## Sugar and Spice, Everything Safe and Nice

**A** nd baby makes three. If there was ever such a simple statement that encompassed so much, this has got to be it. That little bundle of joy coming your way is about to turn your life topsy-turvy in more ways than you can ever possibly imagine.

And while Dr. Spock, Dr. Joyce Brothers, and even Dr. Ruth can fill you in on what it's all going to mean to your psyche—and the baby's—when it comes to the basic task of creating a place for the newest member of the family to live, it's a whole other story.

What you don't know about where your baby is going to spend the first year or two of its life could fill a book. And this is it. Everything you've learned over the years about decorating, furnishing, choosing colors and fabrics, selecting furniture, mixing antiques with new pieces, creating storage, and generally designing a special environment can now basically be tossed aside.

The rules are completely different when it comes to baby rooms. While design and style may have been the most important criteria in decorating your living room or bedroom, they now must take a backseat to some new and much more important considerations: safety and convenience.

That antique dresser, ever so charming and nostalgic, just won't do: the color is all wrong. The family heirloom crib, used by your mother, and hers before, simply isn't safe enough with all we now know. And you might as well give back the pretty floor lamp you practically stole at a garage sale because that electrical cord and top heavy design are basic "no-nos" when it comes to baby's room.

But it isn't just safety you need to be concerned with. Do you have any idea how many diapers Junior is going to go through? And do you realize how much time and energy you'll save if they're stored close to the changing table? You should see the amount of stuffed animals, rattles, plastic toys, and other assorted paraphernalia a one-year-old can accumulate.

You're about to embark on one of the greatest adventures of your life and you'll have your hands pleasantly full bringing up the newest member of the human race. With this book, you can provide your baby with a place to spend his or her first few years that is not only full of "sugar and spice, and everything nice," but that is also a safe and stimulating environment that will grow as your child grows.

9

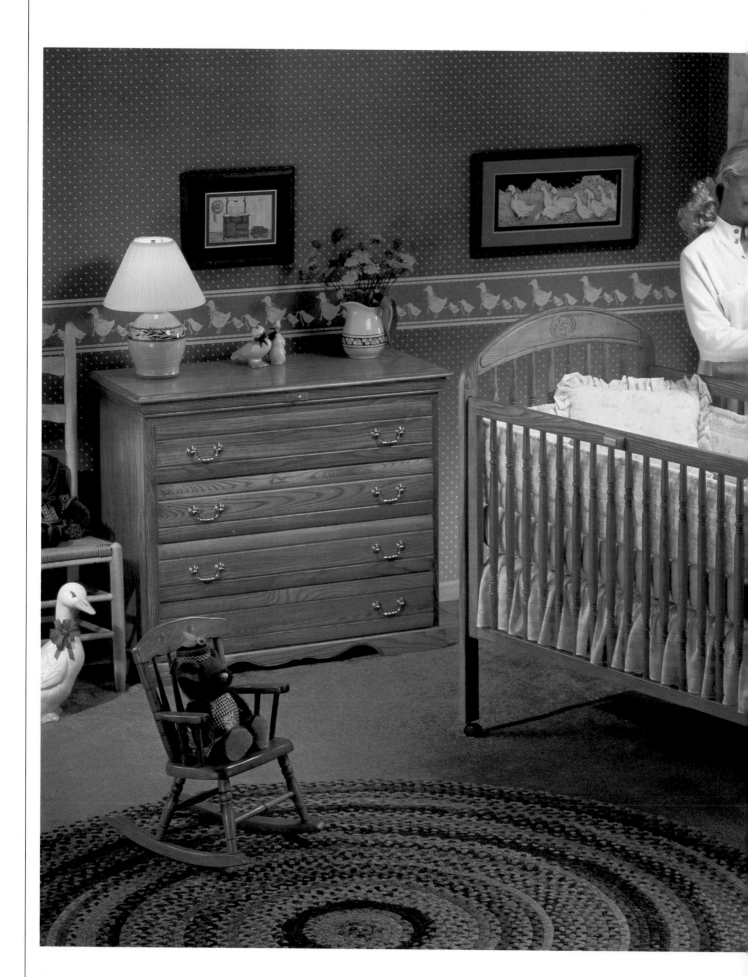

**CHAPTER 1**

# Planning Your Baby's Room

**I**f you really want to know why a baby's room is different from all the other rooms in the house, take this simple test: Get down on your hands and knees and take a look around. What you'll see is quite amazing. Suddenly, the room has become a sea of table and chair legs. Electrical outlets are now at eye level. Most of the decorations in the room are too high to really be seen, and just about everything is way out of scale from your new point of view.

You can stand up and return to adult size now, but that's something your new baby won't be able to do for quite some time. That's why it's important that you have a new perspective, both literally and figuratively, on how to put together the newest room in your home.

## Where to Put Baby's Room

Let's start first with what you have available. Obviously, if you live in a one-bedroom condominium—or a studio apartment—your baby's room is going to be a corner of your own. You can fashion a tidy little nursery with the use of

**Don't be afraid to consider unusual spaces for your baby's room. Small nooks and crannies work great for cribs, providing baby with a snug and secure space.**

Courtesy Puck Children's Furniture

*Left:* Since many babies' rooms eventually become children's rooms, it's best to consider a location in your home that will suit both baby and child.

*Right:* While some people would never consider wall-to-wall carpeting for a baby's room, it has some real advantages in providing a warm and cushioney feeling.

some pretty (and, perhaps, sound-deadening) screens placed to neatly partition off a section of space for a crib and a changing table/dresser. It's a short-term solution, but it will get you started.

But if you've got a bit more space, that's just as well. By the time you add a chair or two, some shelves, a closet, and all the trimmings, nothing short of a full room will do.

Don't worry about that second, third, or even fourth bedroom being too small. That's one of the nicest things about babies: they don't need a lot of headroom. In fact, there's a whole school of thinking that says babies shouldn't be placed in oversized rooms. How would you feel sleeping in the middle of a gymnasium-sized bedroom? Just as in the story of *Goldilocks and the Three Bears,* a room scaled for a child may be "just right."

A crib can look simply charming under a sloping eave where a bed would never work. A cozy little dor-

mer window can be a perfect little nest for a child-sized table and chair set or a rocker. Attic corners, too short for even a chest of drawers, make perfect nooks for low-to-the-ground open shelving or a gaggle of brightly colored storage bins, such as milk crates.

So, don't put up the "For Sale" sign and start mortgage shopping. Chances are, there's a room in your house that's just right for your baby's room.

What if you have a choice of several rooms? Logic dictates that you follow the old rule about keeping the shortest distance between you and a crying baby. That means the closest bedroom to yours should be your baby's. It's a fact of life you'll truly come to appreciate at three o'clock in the morning.

Sometimes things don't always work out exactly the way you want them to, however. Maybe the closest bedroom is right next to your living room and you feel you'd

like to continue having friends over frequently without worrying about the noise level. Maybe the room shares a wall with a noisy neighbor's apartment. Or possibly it's just a dark and dingy room better left for the ironing board and the vacuum cleaner.

If that's the case, it may be better to take the long-range view of things. Those middle-of-the-night feedings are going to stop after a few months anyway. With the new nursery monitors now on the market (see page 72), you can listen in on your baby several rooms, or even several houses, away. And it's important that the nursery be bright, cheery, and able to grow with your child.

So take all these factors into consideration when picking your baby's room. Once you've finished painting, decorating, and putting everything into place, it's a decision you, and your baby, are going to have to live with for some time to come.

# The Inspection

Now that you've narrowed down where your baby's room is going to be, it's time to see what you've got to work with. Before you begin picking out the paint and moving in the crib, you've got to take a look around the basic construction and layout of the room to make sure the stage is properly set for your nursery.

But before you start drawing up plans, take a moment just to put things in the proper time frame. As you've no doubt been told by every parent, doctor, and neighbor around, your baby isn't going anywhere by herself the first few months of her life. You'll decide when she'll be in her crib, when she'll be in her high chair, and when she'll be crawling around her room for at least the first six months. So, many of the baby-proofing steps described here don't absolutely, positively have to be taken in these early planning stages. You have some time before much of this is needed and you may even feel a little foolish doing some of these things so prematurely. (It's a little like putting your snow tires on in September rather than December.)

However, don't wait too long. One day you're going to walk in and see your baby standing up in his crib, when just that morning you thought that would have been impossible. Or you're going to turn your back after setting baby down on the changing table only to find him crawling precariously close to the edge.

So, there's nothing wrong with getting a headstart on making sure your baby's room—and, in fact, the entire house—is baby-proofed.

## Floors and Floor Coverings

Let's begin with the nursery, from the bottom up. What kind of floor are you starting out with? While there are proponents of both carpeted and non-carpeted surfaces, just about everyone agrees that certain floor coverings just won't do. Number one on the "no-no" list is shag carpeting. Thick, bushy carpet hides not only lots of dirt and food crumbs, but also a multitude of small bits and pieces of things just right for the mouth of an inquisitive and teething toddler. The shag has to go.

If you have regular carpeting, you may decide to keep it, but you should weigh the pros and cons. Wall-to-wall

carpeting gives a nice, cozy feel to a room and warms up the whole atmosphere, both figuratively and literally. And it does provide a safer landing surface for toys, glass feeding bottles, and even the well-padded posterior of your baby just learning to walk.

On the other hand, carpeting retains stains, some odors, and a certain amount of dust no matter how good a housekeeper you are. Somewhere along the line you're going to spill something, such as some formula that won't come out completely. And that's not counting what your soon-to-be-three-year-old will be capable of doing with a jar of finger paint or a bowl of tomato soup.

If you do go with carpet, pick a flat, tightly woven, loop-pile design in a synthetic fiber, such as nylon or olefin.

This type resists abrasion and stains better than most and usually holds its color longer. A carpet made up of several shades of the same color may be your best bet for hiding dirt. And don't forget to look for the commercial stain and soil protectors such as Scotchgard™.

If you decide against carpeting, one alternative is wooden floors—the smoother and shinier the better—with perhaps a nice coat of polyurethane. That will really make those toy trucks roll. You can also consider vinyl or linoleum flooring, which are manufactured in many colors and patterns and tend to have a little more bounce than wood.

A nice compromise might be wooden or vinyl flooring topped with a small area rug (don't forget to pick one with a non-skid backing). You can

place the rug in front of baby's crib or underneath a table and chair set. Some manufacturers also make rugs that coordinate with their crib bedding.

## Wall Coverings and Paint

What about the walls around you? Your first step should be to find out what you have on the walls now. Chances are, it's paint, and chances are, that's fine. But if you're in an older house or apartment you have to consider the possibility of lead paint on your walls. It's a serious problem and one that should get top priority.

Lead poisoning, caused when an infant eats even a tiny flaked-off paint chip, can cause a whole host of ailments, including permanent brain damage. If you suspect your house was painted with

Courtesy Fisher-Price

*Above:* **Wallpaper borders—thin strips of paper that wrap around the room—are a terrific way to add a decorative touch to your baby's room. While usually displayed at the tops of walls, they can also be used at mid-wall height.**

*Left:* **Area rugs or small scatter rugs can be a nice accent in a nursery, but always remember to pick ones with a non-skid backing. Use your imagination when it comes to shapes.**

leaded paint at some point in its history, have it checked. You can hire a service that will meter your walls to determine their lead content.

If it's too high, the only real choice is to get rid of all the paint on both the walls and ceiling. You should have it done by a professional, who will take care to remove all the lead residue and dust particles you might miss. All pets and children should be out of the house during the entire time of the removing procedure.

Simply painting over the old lead paint won't make the problem go away, and sooner or later, your walls are going to start flaking again. Just bite the bullet and get the lead out.

Before we talk about what to put back up on the walls, let's continue our inspection. How is the wall space in the room? Is there enough for a crib and a dresser with a

changing table? Both work best against a solid wall and not in front of a window.

And what about those windows? They should have screens to keep out insects and other pests. If you live in a high-rise apartment building, sturdy bars or window guards are an absolute must for all windows throughout your apartment. They may not be attractive but they serve a very real purpose.

Needless to say, cribs and dressing tables should not be positioned directly in front of windows, no matter how nice the light is. Likewise, keep them away from radiators and ducts where the heat or air conditioning may be too strong for sensitive infants. Radiators and baseboard heating elements should have their covers checked (You do have covers on them, don't you?) and resecured if they're loose.

Courtesy Child Safety Products, Inc.

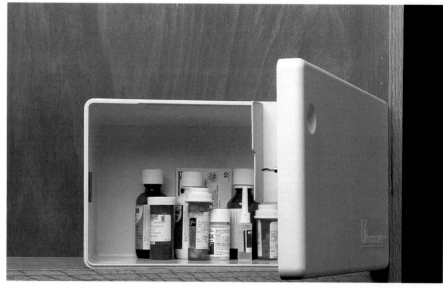

Courtesy Child Safety Products, Inc.

# Baby-Proofing

Now, it's time to check the electrical design of baby's room. Modern codes say there has to be an electrical outlet every six feet (1.8 meters). While that's nice when you want to plug something in, it means that every six feet there's something for a curious crawler to explore and experiment with.

Fortunately, this is one area in baby-proofing where you can be properly armed to deal with the unexpected. There are several different products on the market that will cover up open outlets. Some are clear plastic and hardly noticeable. All of these products are quite effective against tiny prying fingers.

Likewise there are plug guards that will hold in place electrical plugs currently in use. They do the trick quite nicely, yet don't get in the way of everyday use of appliances, clocks, and such. You should also consider a host of other similar products now on the market that perform a variety of functions, such as keeping long electrical cords bunched together and out of the reach of you-know-who.

Most of all, these kinds of simple devices are inexpensive, extremely easy to put on (using the word *install* would be making it sound too complicated), and they blend in easily with any decor. Look upon outlet guards as necessities—not an extra you'll get around to next week—for every outlet in your entire house.

There are a few more steps to baby-proofing your new nursery. Consider doorknob protectors that make it easy for you to open any door (don't forget closets), but will effectively frustrate smaller members of the household who want to explore.

A variety of different cabinet, window, and door locks work in essentially the same manner: Two separate and

*Above left:* **Perhaps the most important part of your home inspection has to do with checking for unsafe conditions. All electrical outlets— and there are probably far more than you ever realized—need to be covered or protected.** *Above right:* **Dangerous medicines and household cleaners need to be put out of your baby's reach. Consider a locking cabinet for inside your medicine chest. Products that help to baby- proof your home are readily available and relatively inexpensive.**

distinct, yet simple, actions are needed to release the lock. It's a piece of cake for you, but out of the league of little ones. These latches are great for kitchen cabinets and drawers, closets, doors to infrequently used rooms, such as basements and attics, and—don't forget—the medicine cabinet. For that dangerous spot in the house, you might consider a locking mini-cabinet within your cabinet where you can store prescription drugs, spare razor blades, and other items you might not use every day.

Spend some time going through your entire home and check everything that opens. Chances are, whatever it is—closet, drawer, cabinet, door, or even the toilet bowl (yes, they make special locks for them, too)—has the potential to be a dangerous adventure for your toddler. Take care of everything in advance, and you won't have to worry about it later.

*Below:* **If your home has more than one level, you will want to be sure and purchase one especially important piece of safety equipment—the door gate. It protects your baby from the stairs to the basement, attic, and such, but can also be used to keep curious crawlers out of certain rooms, such as kitchens and bathrooms.**

Courtesy Fisher-Price

# A Little Local Color

Now that you've done the hard part, the fun starts. Who doesn't like picking out the color scheme for your baby's room? It's one of the nicest chores you'll ever do in your home. But that's not to say it's going to be one of the easiest. You have two very distinct—and very different—routes to take when selecting a color

scheme. The first choice is what we might call "The Technicolor Spectacular," and as you can guess, it highlights the bright, primary colors. Red and blue tend to be dominant colors, but you'll also find that bright yellow and striking green are both a part of the primary palette.

The other side of the coin could be called "Fairy Tale Land," and again, you can figure this one out too: soft, muted pastels in shades of

*Above:* These days, baby's rooms come in all sorts of colors. Vivid primary colors are one route to go, using bright reds and blues in both the furniture and decorative accessories, as well as in the wall coverings. *Right:* On the other hand, there's a case to be made for good old black and white, used for accessories in the nursery. Young infants can't distinguish individual colors but they do respond to contrast, which makes black and white crib toys big news.

Courtesy Turn on Toys, Inc./photo by Teresa Zabala

pink and blues, and more recently, pale mint greens, dusty roses, and creamy mauves.

Each scheme captures an unmistakable feeling and it really comes down to your own personal taste and likes. But there are a few considerations to take into account before you make the choice, and in fact, there's even a case to be made for good old black and white.

Most current research into the subject today says that up to the age of about four or five months, babies cannot see colors. They can distinguish between the brightness of colors, but that smiling face looking up from the crib wouldn't know red from green—and wouldn't care either.

So, that's why, at least in the early stages of your baby's development, it's the contrast in colors that really counts. In fact, at least two different companies have recently introduced black and white crib mobiles and stuffed animals. It's an interesting concept and these kinds of visually stimulating products may likely prove to be quite popular with newborns. But should you paint your new nursery black and white? Probably not. The key criteria here is the relationship of the two shades: Alternating black and white walls don't create the contrasting shapes and patterns that are really important for visual stimulation.

Logic would seem to indicate that the answer then is a room made of bright primary colors, since the contrasts will be much stronger than in a room with pastel shades. And you wouldn't be wrong if this is the route you decide to take.

But if you have your heart set on that Fairy Tale Nursery, then go for it. By the time your baby is six months old, she'll be picking out colors, regardless of which type they are.

More important, however, is the role the room itself plays in the overall design of the nursery. The walls, ceiling, and trim should serve as a backdrop for the total effect. Furniture, toys, curtains, and baby herself are the real stars, and as any movie extra will tell you, the trick is not to upstage the featured players.

A nice compromise to consider is doing something dramatic on just one wall. Keep three walls white or a muted color and then make a splash on the fourth. One fire-engine red wall set against three crisply white surfaces makes a great statement without getting carried away. A little later on we'll talk about alternatives to paint that can also be used in this fashion.

# The Well-Dressed Wall

No matter what color scheme you choose, always keep in mind the average lifespan of this room. Chances are, it's going to be home for not only your baby, but also your toddler, your preschooler, your child, and maybe even your teenager. To keep the painting and redecorating chores to a minimum, it pays to go with as basic and durable a design as possible.

Now that you know some

of the pros and cons, here are a few general tips to keep in mind:

• Latex or plastic-based paints will wear the best in a nursery since they can be easily washed with a sponge and water. Touch-ups, too, are faster and smoother.

• Enamel has a nice shine, too, and can also be sponge-cleaned, but there are those who say it tends to chip more than other paints and that touch-ups are more difficult because enamel is tough to apply evenly.

• Oil-based paints are the old standby, but are the toughest to clean and the most difficult to apply. They are especially practical for woodwork, however.

But don't consider paint your only choice. Wallpaper is also a wonderful alternative. Pick a ''water-resistant'' type. The other kind is called ''water-sensitive'' and that just won't do for your baby's room. You'll find water-resistant paper the easiest to clean and the most durable. Generally, there are part-vinyl or all-vinyl papers, including flocks and foils.

Go with a prepasted backing, if possible; all you need do is dip the wallpaper strip in water and hang it up. You may still need some paste for corners and edges, but this will make it much easier all around.

Like paint, wallpaper can be used for the entire room, or just for a portion of it. Consider, too, wallpaper borders that ring the top of your baby's room giving it a handsome edging. Many of today's manufacturers of infant bedding and decorative accessories offer borders to match their quilt designs, giving you

Courtesy Motif Designs/Wallpaper & Fabric by Marimekko Little People

a totally coordinated look.

And if you want a quick rule of thumb for deciding how many rolls you'll need (they usually come in two-bolt packages, each covering approximately thirty to thirty-six square feet [approximately three square meters] regardless of varying widths and lengths), try this one:

Measure the distance in feet around the room, and the height of the walls to be covered, and multiply the two total figures. Then divide by thirty to get the approximate number of rolls you'll need. Deduct one roll for every two door openings or four windows and that will give you a

rough idea of how much to buy. Keep in mind that it's always better to have a little extra than to run out with one-half wall to go.

Your wallpaper dealer can give you more help and show you as many sample books as you have the time to look at.

Don't forget that our choices don't end there. Wall paneling these days seems to come in almost as many styles and patterns as wallpaper. It's relatively easy to put up, durable for your baby's room, and not that expensive, especially if you decide to do just one wall, for example.

Mirrored walls are another way to go. They're especially practical for small or narrow rooms when used cleverly. One additional avenue you may not have considered is the use of photomurals. You can get a number of off-the-shelf designs, including ocean, forest, and mountain scenes, sunsets, and skylines, but photo processing services, such as those from Eastman Kodak, will also take your color slides and blow them up into murals, complete with rigid backing. The possibilities are really endless.

Stenciling is yet another alternative, especially if you want to achieve a "country look." You can apply stenciling directly on the wall or, if you're not feeling quite sure about the whole thing, you can stencil on sheets or rolls of paper. By the way, stenciling is especially effective on ceilings. Some stenciled (or cut-out) stars and moons set against a pale blue ceiling create an outstanding look.

Finally, we've saved the best for last: murals. A drawn or painted mural probably works better in a nursery than

*Above:* **Stenciling is another great way to decorate walls. If you're not sure you're going to like it, stencil on sheets or rolls of paper that can be removed later on.**

*Facing page:* **Many companies now offer wall coverings that coordinate with crib bedding, making a totally unified look possible. Remember, if you're using an antique in the nursery, such as an old toy chest, it should be retrofitted with new hinges and air holes to meet today's safety standards.**

*Above:* **A mural for your baby's room is the ultimate wall decoration. While some may be too complicated for the do-it-yourselfer, you'd be surprised at what you're capable of doing when you have good guidelines to follow.**

anyplace else in the house. It seems to say baby all over it. And you really don't have to be a professional artist to pull the whole thing off. Instructions for painting a mural follow at the end of this chapter, but let your imagination run wild when it comes to selecting your subject.

Nursery rhymes and more contemporary characters such as Raggedy Ann and Andy and Mickey Mouse come to mind immediately, but don't stop there. Scenes from such classic films as *Fantasia* and *Bambi* could create a unique look. So would a sports scene, such as a baseball stadium.

Again, just remember that babies have a habit of growing up and that in a few years, your four- or five-year-old may not think much of that "baby" painting you did on the wall. But don't let that stop you. Express yourself with a mural that reflects you and your love for your new baby. Go all the way and sign it in the lower right hand corner. You deserve the credit for a job well done.

## A STEP-BY-STEP GUIDE
# How To Create a Mural

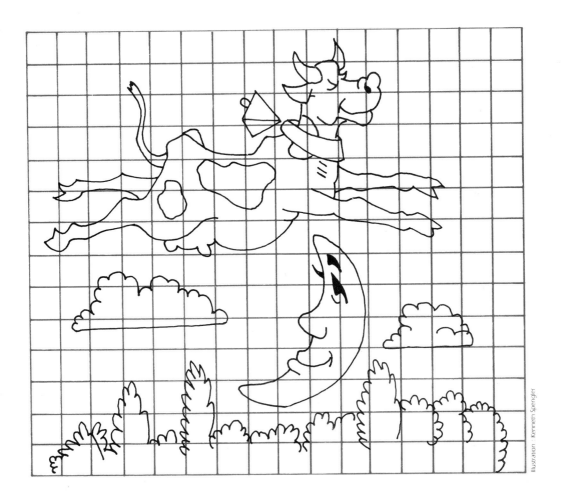

Illustration Kenneth Spengler

The easiest way to paint a mural is to transfer a design from a little format—picture, photograph, small drawing, even a slide projected onto the wall—to a large format through a grid system. Here's the way to go about it.

**1.** After selecting your subject, either draw it on grid paper or draw a grid of squares over the design itself. You'll find it's easiest if each square is between one-half and one inch (approximately two to three centimeters) on a side. Of course, all squares must be the same size.

**2.** With a pencil, lightly draw the same number of squares on the wall, making each box proportionately larger to fill the space. Let a calculator help you out on the math.

**3.** Now, just transfer the art from each little square on your paper to each large box on the wall, using a pencil. But remember not to draw the lines too darkly or your pencil marks will show through the paint.

**4.** It's time to get your paint ready. Latex or alkyd paints are best. The former are water-based, quick drying, and clean up fast, while the latter require turpentine or other chemicals for mixing and cleaning but offer a wider range of colors. Get lots of different brushes ready and have your colors pre-mixed so you

won't have problems matching later.

**5.** Start at the top to avoid drips spoiling your work. Begin with the color that covers the most amount of space, then fill in secondary colors and just keep within your guidelines. Let each color dry and then start the next. Pretty soon, those splotches of color will begin to look like a professionally painted mural.

**6.** After everything is dry, consider putting a thin layer of polyurethane varnish over the whole work. It will bring out the colors and serve as an easy-to-clean coating over your masterpiece. If you've really done a great job, invite the neighbors in and you may be able to start a new career. And don't forget the signature . . . it's the mark of all great artists.

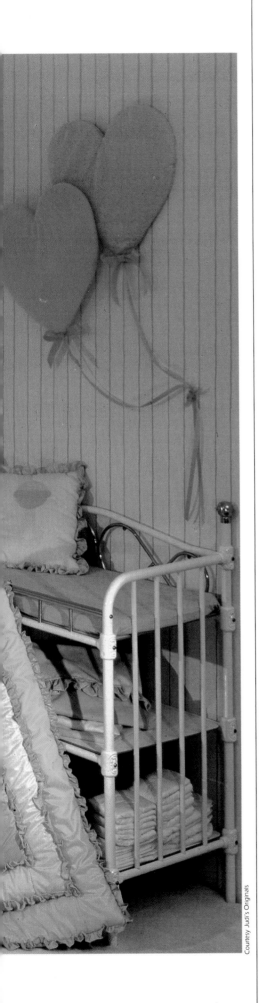

# CHAPTER 2

# Furnishing Your Baby's Room

*Above:* **When planning your baby's room, remember that some cribs with high headboards may require extra head room.**

Courtesy Merryland by Marilyn/Patent Pending

**N**ow that you've finished setting the table—picking the right room, selecting floor coverings, painting, papering, and even doing a spot of fine art—it's time for the main course: the furniture that will really set the tone for your baby's room.

And whether you go with the brand new, the reasonably priced secondhand, or the heirloom antique—an issue we'll tackle shortly—there are a couple of things to do before you get started.

## Paper Training

As with any other decorating project, you'll need some kind of a plan beforehand. We've all heard the stories about the king-sized bed that didn't fit into the bedroom or the piano that wouldn't make it through the doorway. Well, the same thing can happen in a nursery. That crib that looked so darling on the sales floor doesn't fit on the short wall you wanted to place it against. Or that handsome highboy chest of drawers is too tall to fit beneath the window.

So before you make any expensive mistakes, plan it out. The easiest way to do that is on paper. Take a sheet of graph paper and draw out the dimensions of your room to scale. Don't forget to place in all the doors, windows, and closets. If there's an especially low ceiling in part of the room, indicate it.

Now, using the boxes on the graph paper for measuring, cut out the basic pieces of furniture you'll need in the nursery. And since you probably don't already know the measurements of these items (unless you've read this book before), here are some basic dimensions:

**Cribs:** Most are usually about 53 inches (134 centimeters) long by 30 inches (76 centimeters) wide with a height of about 45 to 48 inches (115 to 123 centimeters). These are the averages, remember; the dimensions of antique cribs, cribs that convert to day beds, and cribs with canopies will vary considerably.

**Dressers:** Averages are a little harder to come by with dressers due to styling differences, but you can generally figure 42 to 62 inches (107 to 157 centimeters) long, 18 inches (46 centimeters) deep, and 31 to 36 inches (76 to 78 centimeters) high. Don't forget that you may want to use the top of a dresser as a changing table, so allow for extra height. Freestanding changing tables will run about the same size.

**Chests:** Again, you'll find a wide variety of measurements based on styles—some of those Queen Anne highboys with pediments get pretty high—but usually plan about 32 to 37 inches (79 to 92 centimeters) long, 18 inches (46 centimeters) deep, and 41 to 50 inches (105 to 127 centimeters) high depending on whether the chest has four or five drawers.

**Shelving and Storage:** The sky is the limit here—it all depends on the type of storage unit. About the only constant is that most units will be 18 inches (46 centimeters) deep, although some shelving may only be 12 inches (30 centimeters) deep.

Other furniture items, such as table and chair sets and rockers vary so much that there are no general measurements. But by designing your space for the major pieces, you'll get a better idea of how everything is going to fit.

There's one other way to plan your room on paper, and while it's not nearly as exact-

*Above:* **The furniture for your baby's room comes in a variety of shapes, colors, styles, and sizes. By doing a to-scale floor plan of the space *before* you buy anything, you may save yourself a lot of trouble.**

ing as the first, it does have a certain attraction. Again, draw your room to scale on paper. Then cut out actual pictures of the type of furniture you're going to be using in the room, using magazine ads, catalogs, or your own drawings. If you have a swatch of wallpaper, place that in the background. You can even smear a little paint on the side of your paper floor plan to see how it all looks together.

It's a different kind of way to look at things that will certainly give a new perspective to your planning.

# The Old, New, or Borrowed Blues

Once you've decided the types of furniture you're going to use in your baby's room, it's time to go shopping. And here is where you're going to be making some of your most important—and difficult—decisions.

There are three ways you can obtain the furniture for your nursery. Each has its advantages and its drawbacks. Chances are, you'll settle on some combination of the three. The trick is to find the right balance.

## Brand, Spanking New

Nothing beats new, except for possibly new and free. Unless the grandparents are going to foot the bill, the only way to get new is to pay for it.

And in many cases, it's all worth it. You'll be getting the very newest, most up-to-date styles, state-of-the-art construction and hardware, and the full backing of the retailer and manufacturer selling the product. Perhaps most important, there'll be no worries about whether the product meets the latest safety standards for sizing, paint content, etc. What you're buying for the most part is peace of mind.

It may not come cheap, however. Although furniture remains one of the better values in consumer products today (prices have increased relatively little compared with such products as automobiles or clothing), a three-piece nursery ensemble (crib, dresser, and chest) is still going to set you back a pretty penny if you go for anything above the most basic level.

The old maxim about getting what you pay for clearly applies to nursery furniture. You can buy new furniture at a number of places. Most cribs and coordinating furniture is bought at juvenile furniture specialty stores, those smaller stores you're likely to find in shopping centers or on a main shopping street of your town. They specialize in these products and tend to have the widest selection around. You're also likely to find the most informed sales people in specialty stores.

Toy "supermarkets," such as Toys"R"Us and Child World, also carry a big selection of furniture and have competitive prices. Discount stores, such as K mart, Wal-Mart, or Target, will have a smaller offering but again the prices will be good. The big national chain stores, Sears,

Courtesy Noel-Joanna, Inc.

Courtesy Child Craft, Inc.

*Above:* **Some baby furniture converts into children's furniture, such as this crib that can be changed into a youth bed. While units like this tend to be a more expensive initial investment, they can save money in the long run.**

*Left:* **Buying new furniture for your baby allows you to choose matching pieces and gives you the peace of mind in knowing that everything meets existing safety standards.**

Roebuck & Co., J. C. Penney, and Montgomery Ward's, will also have a large assortment.

Depending on where you live there may be several other types of stores worth checking out, including catalog showrooms (such as Service Merchandise and Best Products) and warehouse membership clubs (such as The Price Club and Pace). These stores will offer excellent prices but little or no personal service.

While there are some mail-order companies selling products for your baby (don't forget the Sears and J. C. Penney's catalogs), most specialize in smaller accessory items and will have limited selections of furniture.

One type of store you should probably pass up when it comes to buying baby furniture is the department store. As part of an overall move away from larger and slower moving lines and towards more apparel and fashion accessories, department stores, such as Macy's, May

Co., and Broadway Stores, have essentially gotten out of the baby furniture business.

## Used, Slightly or Otherwise

Whether it's a hand-me-down from your sister or a bargain at a garage sale, getting used baby furniture remains one of the most popular ways to furnish your nursery. And well it should. Unlike a 1958 DeSoto or that toaster oven that always started with a little puff of smoke, used furniture is basically a "what you see is what you get" proposition. With even a casual inspection of a piece, you can tell how sturdy it is, how the finish has held up, and if it's been involved in any less-than-desirable situations, ranging from floods to being left outdoors, to getting caught in the middle of the gunfight at the OK Corral.

Chances are, much of the used furniture you're likely to run into will be in pretty good shape. Americans are having fewer children these days, which means the days of a crib being used by all six of the Brady Bunch are pretty much over. One or two children, using a chest of drawers for even ten years, can't have done too much damage, especially if you're handy with some touch-up stain and a nail or two.

One additional plus for used furniture is that nursery furniture does not tend to change styles every season or even every year. Darker wood colonial or early American furniture, and contemporary, European-influenced styles in lighter shades of oak, and painted surfaces have been the most popular styles for a number of years, so you're likely to find what you want out there if that's the way your tastes run. You'll only have a problem if you want to buy a more unusual style of furniture, such as one in French provincial or American Empire.

Obviously the best thing overall about used furniture is the price. Cribs and dressers can be picked up for one-tenth their original price at a garage sale, and that is a tempting deal when you remember what the obstetrician is charging you.

Again, however, you get what you pay for. Especially when considering a crib, you must make sure it meets all current safety standards. Most were adopted in 1974 (see page 110 for full details), but some regulations are more recent. Unfortunately, cribs usu-

*Courtesy Petco Prints, Kidsprints™*

*Above:* **Your baby is going to need plenty of storage space for all her things. Toy chests, shelves, and hooks all provide great solutions, whether you add new pieces or use existing elements.**

*Right:* **Antiques can make a baby's room a very special place—but only if they're the right pieces. Before you use just any old piece of furniture, make sure it meets current safety regulations. Pretty is nice, but safe is nicer.**

ally don't carry the date when they were manufactured, so unless you carry around a copy of the Federal Register in your back pocket you may not be sure you're getting the safest there is.

Also, there may be some concern whether you want a crib with some other baby's teething marks on it. It's more psychological than physical, but to some people that's a real turn-off.

Finally, there's the "Prince and/or Princess Syndrome." Chances are, you're having this baby a little later in life than your parents had you. You may both be working and you may be bringing in a bit more "take-home" salary than the generation before you. This is your first baby and she is going to have everything she wants, it's going to be the best available on the market, and, what the heck, that's what they invented credits cards for anyway.

No matter how you feel about used furniture, you should at least take a look at what's out there. Garage or tag sales, as mentioned, are probably your best bet, but also look in your local newspaper's "merchandise offerings" or "furniture for sale" classified listings. You might also check flea markets or second-hand furniture stores in your area.

And don't forget your cousin's basement. Tucked away in the corner, behind that old washing machine, next to the luggage with no handle and the tuba no one's played since

1963, you're just likely to find the perfect changing table for your new nursery.

## The Older, the Better

When you hit a golden oldie, you can really strike pay dirt. Who hasn't dreamed of a brass Victorian crib for their baby, decked out with fine silk lace bunting? Doesn't the idea of converting that antique armoire into a storage unit for a nursery sound charming? And what about taking the old sewing machine table from your grandmother's attic and remaking it into a changing table?

These are all great ideas and all of them will work, too—in certain circumstances. In others, however, they could spell disaster. The very things that make antique cribs so splendid—their graceful curves, intricate ironwork, and unique

dimensions—are also, unfortunately, the same factors that can make them extremely unsafe. Uneven spacings, head or limb-trapping nooks and crannies, and ill-fitting mattresses can all lead to tragedy.

And while cribs represent the most serious danger, other furniture can also present problems. Lead paint used on old dressers and chests is just as much a health hazard as older painted walls. Likewise, a changing table without the proper restraining device can cause a safety hazard once your baby learns to move around a little bit.

It isn't just a matter of safety concerns with antiques, either. Take that changing table converted from a sewing machine table, circa 1900. The ironwork is outstanding, and the patina of the wood is warmly aged and enchanced. But it's just too low. After a

Courtesy Laura Ashley

*Courtesy Judi's Originals*

few changing sessions, either your chiropractor's going to be picking up some additional business or the sewing machine table is going back to Grandma's house.

Today's cribs, while they may not have the historical significance of a real Victorian piece, may be better suited for your brand of living. New cribs feature dropsides for easily getting your baby in and out. The mattress support is adjustable, so that as your baby grows up her mattress can be gradually lowered, extending the life of the product. And they accept standard-size crib mattresses, not exotic shapes and sizes that may have to be custom-built.

Still the allure of an older piece is awfully tempting. You

can use antiques, but you have to be extra careful and diligent when outfitting them for use today. One antique piece in an otherwise contemporary nursery may be just the eclectic balance you're looking for.

If the call of antiques remains strong, your best bet may be shows and markets that specialize in antique furniture. If at one particular show no one has baby furniture, ask around and you'll probably get a dozen referrals. Classified ads and conventional flea markets and garage sales are a longer shot, but the potential is always there to find that one piece you've always wanted. Such is the stuff dreams are made of . . . and some baby's rooms, too.

*Above:* **A great compromise for your nursery might be combining the new with the old: a state-of-the-art crib with an antique storage unit. Wicker, too, works great in a baby's room.**

*Right:* **The crib is the starting point for furnishing any baby's room. Cribs come in a variety of styles and colors, including some with intricate carvings and canopies.**

Courtesy Child Craft, Inc.

# Getting Down to Basics

Before you throw your hands up in exasperation and ask, "What's A Parent To Do?," remember that each method of obtaining pieces for your baby's room has its merits and will work. So, regardless of where you end up getting your nursery furniture, it's time to start shopping. Here are rundowns on the basic items you'll need and the individual features and safety concerns to be on the lookout for.

## Cribs

This is the most basic of the nursery basics and, as such, the first thing you should obtain for your baby's room. All else will follow. Your first decision is whether you want your crib to match the rest of the furniture or be a free-standing piece that blends or even contrasts with the rest of the key furnishings in the room. The choice is yours and essentially it's a case of personal preference.

Occasionally, you'll fall in love with a crib that doesn't have matching case pieces (the trade name for such furniture items as dressers or chests), but usually a particular style will be offered in all major pieces. The one exception is if you select a crib made of brass or a brass and iron combination. In that one construction, the crib is usally the only item offered.

Most new cribs, however, are wood, or more accurately a wood veneer, often with some plastic parts, over lesser material such as particle board or chip board. Most are finished in a certain wood grain —oak, mahogany, walnut, or pine—but again it's just a finish and in most cases you're not actually getting a crib made of that particular wood. Painted surfaces—usually white, or more recently bright primary blues and reds as well as softer almonds and pastels—are also available.

Styles also run the gamut when it comes to wooden cribs. The single most popular style for the past several years is a model made by many manufacturers that features carved slats (what most people call bars) on all four sides. For some reason that no one seems to really understand, it's called a Jenny Lind, after the popular nineteenth century European singer.

Most other cribs, regardless of the style, usually have solid head and footboards, and slats only on the long sides.

Other leading styles are clean, contemporary cribs, sometimes imported from Italy but more often "Italian-inspired," with natural oak or painted white finishes. Early American or colonial styles also remain strong sellers, but you'll generally find cribs available in almost any style adult furniture is offered in, save for the most avant-garde.

Several years back, however, one company came into the market with a crib that featured a real fish tank in the headboard. The thinking was that it gave a newborn a constantly moving show to watch, better than any mobile or crib toy. Apparently all parents could see was the possibilities of leaking water, wet gold fish on their baby's heads, and even worse. That

particular product, to quote *The Godfather*, "now sleeps with the fishes."

Today's alternatives to traditional wood cribs are brass, usually brass-plated, which is more durable, but can't be easily resurfaced if scratched, and brass/iron combinations; laminate-faced cribs, another durable finish that comes in some interesting colors; metal cribs, usually in bold, shiny colors; and wicker and/or rattan, which often have wood slats.

What do you look for in a crib, especially if you're not into goldfish? Certainly, the fit and finish of the wood are important, and while ease of assembly (yes, they all come unassembled) might be important, most retailers, except for the big discount stores, will

deliver and set up your crib for a minimal charge.

Most cribs feature sides that can be raised and lowered, hence the name dropside. Often, a crib will have double dropsides, which sounds nice, but if you're planning on putting the crib against a wall, you'll only need a movable dropside on one side. Double dropsides come under the heading of "bells and whistles," an industry term for a product feature that probably isn't necessary.

Regardless of how many dropsides there are, each is operated by a mechanism that requires two separate and distinct actions: easy for you, but difficult for your baby to do accidently. Each crib manufacturer has designed the mechanism differently, so check out

Courtesy Welsh Juvenile Products

*Right:* Brass cribs—actually most are only brass plated—are a nice focal point in any nursery. Some cribs come in brass/iron combinations for an especially distinctive look.

*Courtesy Lullabye Garden/Crib furnished by Swan Brass Beds/photo by Zev Manor*

*Facing page:* Dark wood, light wood; painted wood or stained; even decals and laminates: You can get a crib in just about any finish imaginable.

which one feels right to you on the floor models. It is, after all, something you're going to be using quite often for the next two to three years.

Cribs will also have adjustable mattress supports, so you can lower the level of the mattress as your baby gets bigger. Again, there are different design answers to this problem, so take a look beneath the mattress to see which design best suits your needs.

When you look at the bottom of some cribs, you may find a bonus: a wide drawer for storage. Only some models have this extra feature—especially nice for storing extra linens and blankets or crib toys—but it's one to look for.

If you're buying a new crib, it has to meet all current federal safety standards, most of which were issued in 1974. (A full rundown of all the current safety standards for cribs and other juvenile products is included on pages 109–111.)

If, on the other hand, your crib is not new, there are several things to check before you use it. If it has the original factory paint on it and it appears to be less than ten years old, there's no need to worry about leaded paint. The current standard for lead content in paint went into effect in early 1978. However, if it appears to have been repainted by a previous owner, you should have the lead content checked by an inspector. Better yet, consider passing on this item and looking for another. It's a risk that isn't worth taking.

If you're going to paint the crib itself, remember to check that your paint was manufactured after February, 1978 and let it dry thoroughly before using the crib so there are no residual fumes.

The second thing to check is the distance between slats. They should be 2⅜ inches or less (about three adult finger widths [approximately one centimeter]) apart. Any larger space can present entrapment or strangulation dangers. This is a critical measurement, and again, if your used crib doesn't meet it—or worse, has missing slats—keep looking for a better crib. The federal government says if you must use a crib with slats spaced further apart, use securely attached bumper pads, those vinyl or cloth pads used to provide a cozier atmosphere for babies, around the entire crib.

Speaking of bumpers, make sure you secure them with snaps or at least six straps and

Courtesy Welsh Juvenile Products

trim the excess off of the straps so they aren't a chewing or entrapment hazard later on. And as soon as your baby can stand up, get rid of the bumpers as they make a great step ladder for baby escapees.

The crib mattress must fit snugly into the crib on all four sides. If you can fit more than two fingers between the edge of the mattress and the crib side, then your mattress is too small and it should be replaced. Large towels can be used to stuff the space in an emergency, but a new mattress is really the only logical solution. And you'll find a new crib mattress to be a

pretty good idea even if the old one looks all right. Most are designed for fairly short lifespans, so a ten-year-old used mattress may not be everything it should be.

A new mattress is not that expensive, at least compared to some other products you'll be buying, so it's a reasonable purchase to make. You'll find crib mattresses in most of the same styles as adult models, from coil spring to all foam, and even water mattresses. The last has proved to be quite successful in hospital use with premature babies and now several companies are making crib-sized water mattresses.

The mattress should be at least twenty-two inches below the top of the rail of the dropside when the mattress is in its lowest position. If it's less, chances are, an active baby will be able to climb over the rail and that's really inviting injuries. By the way, as soon as your baby can stand, all large toys should be removed from inside the crib, as they provide excellent stepping stones out of the crib.

One other area to examine in a used crib is the design of the headboard and footboard. Some older styles have handsome Chippendale-type pediments or maybe even a charming little crescent moon cut-out. Unfortunately, these openings present very real strangulation hazards for small heads. In fact, the federal government warns against any crib post being more than ⅝ inches (¾ centimeters) higher than the rest of the head or footboard. (A canopied bed, of course, is high enough not to present this danger.)

Some offensive posts or decorative elements can be unscrewed or even sawed off, but if you do so, your bargain crib is going to look cheap—rather than inexpensive—so beware of the hazards some older cribs represent.

*Above:* **Furniture manufacturers have become especially creative these days, combining all sorts of materials—here wood and brass—to come up with fresh looks. All cribs on the market today must meet federal safety standards.**

*Facing page:* **The Jenny Lind is perhaps the single most popular crib style. Whether the real nineteenth century Swedish singer ever used one herself is still a mystery. Remember, Jenny Lind is a style made by many companies, not a brand name.**

*Above:* **Your baby's dresser may be with her long after she leaves the crib, so don't get locked in to a "babyish" design when picking out furniture. A hand-painted one can work well into the teenage years.**

# Dressers and Chests

Some people believe chests and dressers absolutely have to match a crib. Others feel that complementing pieces work best. Some probably haven't given it any thought one way or the other.

Whatever your preference, when it comes time to pick out a chest and dresser, there are a few things to keep in mind. Unlike the crib that your baby will outgrow within two

or three years, a dresser or chest may be with her all the way though her teenage years. That cute pink chest with the bunny decals may be adorable right now but when she's 14 and dressing like the latest rock star, she may not be too crazy about it. Decide how long you're going to use the furniture before you buy it.

That's why you may want to check out the local adult furniture store, as well as your juvenile furniture store. Teenage-sized and styled furniture may work quite nicely in the nursery yet still grow with your child. They may even provide some extra storage for you in the first few years when those little baby playsuits won't be taking up all that much space. Of course you'll pay more for such furniture initially, but in the long run it could represent a savings. Again, decide how you're going to be using your furniture and then proceed.

Do you really need a chest and a dresser? The answer can be a resounding no, an emphatic yes, or perhaps a definite maybe. It all depends on your room size and the number and size of closets available for your baby's needs and your budget. Often, a dresser will hold a changing table on its top, which gives you a good dual-function piece of furniture. That's why if you're pressed for space (and cash) and only going to get one or the other, a dresser makes more sense.

But don't underestimate the need for a chest either. It may

Courtesy Motif Designs/Wallpaper & Fabric by Marimekko Little People

*Left:* When furniture shopping, look for the same quality features you would for adult pieces: dovetail joints, drawer liners, and such. But remember that since some baby furniture isn't expected to last as long as adult pieces, it may not be built quite as well.

be the only other surface in the room to place a nursery lamp, a prized baby knick-knack, or a nursery monitor. And that extra storage space can come in handy as your baby goes through a new clothing size every three months for the first few years.

As with cribs, the corresponding case pieces (chests, dressers, and sometimes night tables and armoires) are offered in a variety of styles, finishes, and designs. Wood is the most popular material, but you'll also find metal furniture, laminate-covered pieces, and wicker styles as well. Even if an item is made of wood, chances are it will have a laminate or plastic top, which is the best thing for all around durability and easy clean-up.

Dressers usually have at least three wide drawers, while chests will sport four or five. Each may also substitute a doored storage area for some of the drawers. Armoires will generally have some combination of drawers and closed storage space with either open shelves or room to hang up clothes inside.

As with any furniture, there are several signs of quality to watch for. Dovetail drawers feature interlocking joints and are much sturdier than pieces just glued or nailed together. Likewise, drawers with a center guide (plastic is the usual material these days) tend to slide easier and operate longer than those supported just on either end. Some expensive furniture features a thin piece

of wood between each drawer, to protect against dust and to prevent clothing from falling out of the back of drawers and to the bottom of the piece. It's a nice feature to look for in a dresser or chest.

If you're getting a used dresser or chest, you can look for the same features. There are no specific safety standards relating to these products, other than the obvious one for leaded paint. It can't be said enough times: If you think there's a chance furniture has been painted with lead paint, you must either strip all the paint off or not use that piece of furniture in the nursery. Those are your only choices. Painting over a layer of leaded paint does not solve the problem.

# Changing Tables

Often, your changing table will be the top of your dresser so you won't need a separate piece of furniture. But you may just feel a changing table is a nice extra to have. It's another example of your budget and your available space having the final say.

Changing table styles and materials are all over the spectrum. The usuals—wood, laminates, metals, and wickers (an old standby in this category)—are all there, but there are also some newer, more interesting styles around. PVC (polyvinyl chloride) tubing, such as the type you see in outdoor furniture, is starting to become available, as are some other plastics. You'll find some unusual shapes, textures, and colors in the new plastic changing tables.

Whatever changing surface you settle on—and there's nothing saying you can't use a fold-up vinyl pad on the floor if you want to—remember that manufacturers have put that safety strap there for a purpose. One day, way before you realize it, that cute, but basically non-movable baby of yours is going to learn how to roll over. You'll want to be prepared by safely securing him with the strap.

Courtesy The Little Tikes Company

*Above:* **Changing tables come in two basic varieties: a separate piece of furniture, or just the changing surface to be placed on top of a dresser.**

*Facing page:* **Some baby furniture is designed to be used through young adulthood...and beyond. This crib converts to a youth bed then to a sofa. The matching case pieces are also convertible.**

Photographs (3): Courtesy Child Craft, Inc.

# Convertible Furniture

While you've been reading the various product descriptions so far, the thought has probably occurred to you that a lot of nursery furniture becomes obsolete in a relatively short period of time. You may even have asked yourself why they don't have furniture that can still be used when your baby grows up.

Relax. Somebody—in fact, a lot of somebodies—had the same idea a while ago. The first generally recognized and nationally distributed product considered to be truly convertible was an item called the Crib'N'Bed, made by an American manufacturer named Child Craft. The product, which is still available, features a crib and small chest of drawers sitting on a platform.

When your baby outgrows the crib, the side panels are removed, the chest taken off the platform, and suddenly, you have room for a youth-sized (that's just a little bit smaller than a conventional twin-sized) mattress. The chest can be used independently while some of the crib sides are incorporated into the youth bed's head and footboards.

It was a neat idea then and it remains a very viable item today. However, like many similar products that followed it into the market, it also carries a tidy little price tag, twice as much as some mid-priced crib-only models. Of course you're

Courtesy Cosco, Inc.

getting a lot of furniture for the money, but it's an economic commitment that can be a little overwhelming when you consider all your other baby-related bills.

You're also committing yourself style-wise for a period of as long as ten years. It's a bit of a gamble that you and your soon-to-be-very-opinionated child are going to like that style down the road. Nevertheless, the idea of getting the maximum use out of your purchasing dollar is a tempting one, so take a look at the crib

and bed combinations now on the market and then decide.

Since the first products along these lines came out, a host of other related items has appeared. Some changing tables can be converted to desks, others to storage units for a teenager's room or the den. By the time you read this, no doubt there will be other convertible products in retail stores. They make some solid economic sense, but that initial investment can put off some people. They deserve your consideration.

*Above and right:* **Convertible furniture now comes in a wide variety of styles. This crib converts into a day bed. The cubes of the changing table can be split up into individual modules to be used as night tables, for instance.**

# Cradles and Bassinets

Probably no products are as romantically linked with babies as are cradles and bassinets. Each is essentially a little bed to be used by a baby up until about the age of three months, or until a baby starts to be mobile on its own.

Cradles tend to rock and more closely resemble a miniature wooden crib, while bassinets are almost always made of wicker and sheathed in lace. The nice thing about either product is that it can be placed in your bedroom, so that those middle-of-the-night feeding sessions go faster.

From your baby's point of view, a cradle or bassinet is the right size for his first few months. Cribs can be awfully spacious and intimidating places for a twenty-four-inch little person.

However, in all honesty, you can easily do without either product. Their very short lifespan and lack of an alternative use classify them as luxuries. But their convenience— even for that short period of time—and their out-and-out charm make either item one of the nicest, and most necessary, luxuries you can buy for you and your baby.

If you decide to use a bassinet or cradle, check the manufacturer's instructions for guidelines on how long your baby can use the product. A baby that's too heavy can come crashing through the bottom of a cradle designed for a lighter infant. And an active big baby could tip over or even climb out of a cradle or bassinet.

Since these products tend to be less sturdily constructed than more durable nursery items, you should pay special attention to screws and bolts, periodically checking them to make sure they are tight. Also check leg locks to ensure they are properly engaged when baby is in the product.

*Above:* **The nicest thing about cradles and bassinets is that you can put them in your room during baby's first few months, when those midnight feedings are a regular occurence.**

*Right:* **What you may forget in all the excitement of picking out cribs and other furnishings is that you'll be spending a lot of time in that nursery yourself. Make sure there's a comfortable place for you to sit: a rocking chair is just perfect.**

# Don't Forget Your Place in Baby's Room

In future chapters we'll be looking at other products you'll need for your nursery—the next chapter is all about storage—but one more item just about qualifies as a necessity for your baby's room. And it's for you, not your baby.

You're going to be spending a large part of the next two years of your life in your baby's room. Whether you're feeding or nursing your baby, cradling him to sleep or talking to him, you'll be in that room for hours at a time some days . . . and nights. Many parents don't realize that when furnishing the nursery and as a result, they leave out a very important element in the room: a place to sit down.

And for that purpose, absolutely nothing beats a rocking chair. Pick a massive oak one or a delicate Windsor style, but get yourself a rocker. It will soon be the most comfortable spot in the house for feeding, having a heart-to-heart conversation with your baby, or just watching him sleep. And let's face it: You can't rock your baby to sleep without a rocker.

Best of all, when you've outgrown the need for a rocking chair in the nursery, just pick it up and move it to the family room, the living room, or even your bedroom. It's the kind of family heirloom item you'll grow quickly attached to; just looking at it will conjure up some of the nicest memories you're likely to have about the time when your baby really was a baby.

Courtesy Motif Designs/Wallpaper by Marimekko Little People

## A STEP-BY-STEP GUIDE
# How to Build a "Murphy" Changing Table

With the number of times you're going to be diapering your baby, a changing table really can't be considered anything but a critical necessity.

Often, however, the necessary room just isn't there. Cribs, chests, rockers, doors, windows—they all take up a lot of space. One solution

might be what I call the Murphy changing table, after the famous beds that fold out of the wall. Here's how you can build one for your baby:

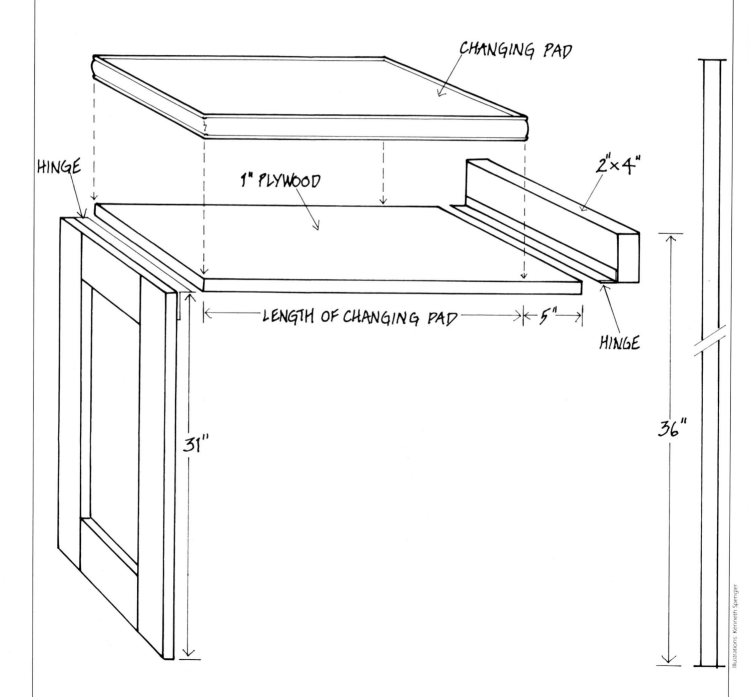

CHANGING PAD

HINGE

1" PLYWOOD

2"x4"

HINGE

|← LENGTH OF CHANGING PAD →|← 5" →|

31"

36"

Illustrations: Kenneth Spengler

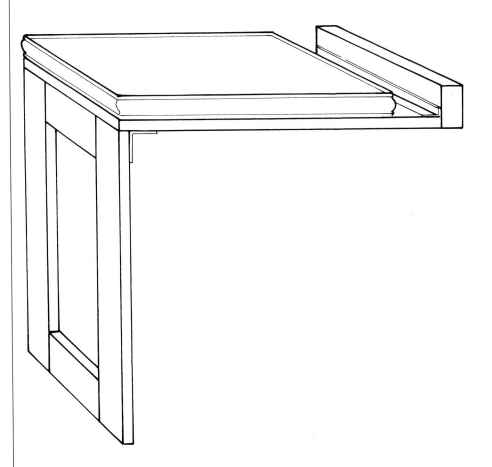

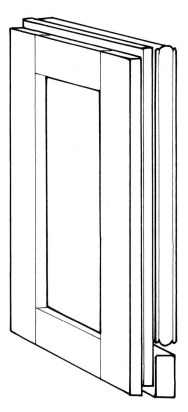

**1.** Locate a wall space about 18 inches (45 centimeters) wide that has about four feet (1.2 meters) of clearance in front of it. Purchase a free-standing changing pad, with safety strap, at a baby products store. This will help you measure out the surface you'll need.

**2.** Cut a piece of two-by-four lumber the width of the changing pad. Secure this to the wall horizontally, with toggle bolts, 36 inches up from the floor, with the top of the two-by-four at the 36-inch mark.

**3.** Cut a piece of one-inch (2.5-centimeter) plywood the length and width of the changing pad. This will be the support for the pad. Cut four strips of one-inch (2.5-centimeter) plywood: two 36 inches (approximately one meter) long, the other two 14 inches (35 centimeters) long, and all four inches (10 centimeters)

in width. These will be used as the support legs for your changing pad when it's in use.

**4.** Purchase a heavy-duty piano-type hinge and secure it to the plywood and the two-by-four wall support. Using a second similar hinge, connect the other end of this piece of wood to the support leg, which is a box made up of the four pieces of wood you previously cut.

**5.** Paint all wooden surfaces, choosing the same color as the wall or going with a contrasting shade, perhaps a vivid primary color. Don't forget to paint the undersides of everything since they will show when the changing table is not in use.

**6.** Attach the changing pad to the wooden surface using Velcro fasteners. This will keep the pad in place yet allow for removal for cleaning or

replacement. Because of the two-by-four support, there will be room for the two-inch (five-centimeter) high pad when your table is folded flat against the wall. Use a hook and eye-type latch to keep the table secured against the wall.

**7.** On the underside of the table surface, tack on some nylon mesh bags of varying sizes. They will lie flat against the table when it's folded up, but will drop down when the table is down. They can hold baby powder, spare diapers, and pins in closed containers.

Your Murphy changing table will drop down and be firmly supported when you need it, but will compactly fold nearly flat against the wall out of the way the rest of the day.

# CHAPTER 3

# Storage

*Courtesy Taylor-Made Creations*

*Above:* **That new little bundle of joy is going to go through nearly a dozen diapers a day, so have an accessible place to put them all. A wall-mounted dispenser is one idea.**

*Facing page:* **Baby clothes are cute, but they don't last very long. You may be storing two, three, or even four different sized wardrobes at any given time, so look for maximum storage space in every piece of furniture you put in baby's room.**

hances are, when you first begin planning the storage space in your baby's room, all you can think about is hanging up those adorable little snowsuits and play sets. And make no mistake about it: they are adorable and they are little. But they're also the least of your worries.

You are about to have a case of the "DD's". The disposable diaper is probably the single greatest convenience item ever invented for parents. Let's face it: This is definitely a product made with the parent's—not the baby's—needs in mind. It should be noted here that recently many people have begun to question the use of disposable diapers. Besides retaining moisture, the plastic surrounding the absorbent material in the diaper does not allow the baby's skin to breathe, thus causing a greater incidence of skin irritations. Environmentalists are also concerned about the harm disposable diapers do to the environment, as they do not decompose. But, it's not ease of changing that concerns us here: it's ease of storing the diapers.

One little Luv's barely takes up any room in the drawer. A pair of Pampers can easily fit into your pocket book. And three or so Huggies can be neatly stowed on any closet shelf. But even put together, those six disposable diapers will last only until about two o'clock this afternoon.

Your newborn baby is going

Courtesy Pat Higdon Industries

to go through almost a dozen diapers a day for the first month or so of her life; that's nearly two boxes a week. And since you're not going to the supermarket every day anymore, you'll probably be buying disposables in bulk whenever the price is right—and the coupons are plentiful. But, think about storing five or six thirteen-inch color television sets in that little nursery you're creating. That's the kind of storage problem you're going to have when it comes to disposable diapers. That's why

you've got to take into account everything your baby is going to be wearing (even if it's only for half an hour) and using when considering storage space in the nursery.

And if you're going to be using cloth diapers instead of disposables, don't for a minute think you're off the hook. Remember that diaper services do pick up and drop off diapers. Thus, you will need only enough storage space for the diapers you will be using.

You have to consider all the other things your baby's room

is about to accumulate. If you're like many couples, you've probably been saving every stuffed animal and plush toy since when you were dating. And they're all earmarked for the baby.

Plush won't be your baby's only toys either. It used to be that infant toys meant rattles and a couple of teething shapes. Now, toys for your baby come in nearly as many sizes, designs, and styles as those for older children. If you've got a big family, a lot of friends and co-workers, or a generous heart, be prepared for the onslaught.

Then there's bedding: One of the reasons the crib looks so charming is the various sets of bedding you have for it: a comforter or two, maybe three crib blankets, and a half-dozen or so crib sheets. And, if you're like many people, you can forget about storing all of that in your already overtaxed linen closet.

Let's not forget about those cute baby clothes either. They are little, but they also have an amazingly short lifespan. Every three to six months, your little one will be getting a little less little and that means going up one size. A baby may only have a limited wardrobe in any one age range, but his closet may contain clothes for two, three, or even more size periods.

In short, your baby may come into this world without a stitch of clothing or a single possession, but in no time he's loaded with "stuff," and all of it has to go somewhere.

# Building or Buying

You're probably not quite up to the task of building a dresser and a crib would certainly be out of the question, but a storage unit, now, that's a different story. Just about every American household has some kind of shelving unit that's homemade, even if there isn't a right angle anywhere to be seen.

Building storage space remains the quintessential do-it-yourself project. You don't have to be a Mr. Fix-It to tackle many storage projects. Open shelving requires little more than attaching some boards to a vertical surface. Even seemingly more complicated projects such as toy chests aren't really that tough when you get right down to it.

As with any household project, know your limitations before you get started. If your patience comes all unglued when you put in your first crooked nail, or if putting in crooked nails is your specialty, then maybe the do-it-yourself route isn't for you.

But if, on the other hand, you can measure wood, handle a saw, and put a few nails into the wall without removing any of your fingers, then building storage for your baby's room may be for you. Consider the advantages.

First, and maybe foremost, is the obvious: saving money. You can build shelving or a wall unit or a toy chest for a fraction of what they would

Courtesy Clarson International

*Above:* With the various storage organizers now out on the market, closets can be customized for optimum storage design. Such kits are inexpensive and easy to assemble, even for the ten-thumbs type.

*Facing page:* Storage bins, boxes, and containers can all be coordinated by using extra sheets from your crib bedding group, cut to fit.

cost to buy. Keep that in mind when you've hit your thumb with the hammer for the twelfth time. In addition to being among the simpler do-it-yourself tasks, building storage also allows you to fit pieces into what would have been wasted space. Those hard-to-fit areas under staircases and beneath sloping ceilings can suddenly and easily be transformed into valuable storage space. You'd never find the right pieces ready-made if you searched in a hundred stores.

Also consider the value of home-built storage over the years. Your open shelving may prove to stand the test of time far better than the unit adorned with nursery rhymes. You can build something that's non-gender-specific or can easily be transformed from a "boy-theme" to one more suitable for a girl. A store-bought piece might not allow you that freedom.

Finally, there's the satisfaction that "I did it." Just as with painting your own wall mural, (see page 25), there's a great deal to be said for having your own personal touch added to your baby's room. You may not be able to sign the toy chest with your signature, but who would know if you carved your initials on the bottom somewhere.

A do-it-yourself project is described at the end of this chapter, covering a common type of storage for you to build: an open-shelved wall unit. Follow the plans or use them as a starting point for your own imagination, adapting them

for specific areas and uses in your baby's room.

Then, of course, there's buying and if you've got the cash—or the plastic—buying certainly has its advantages, too. First and foremost, there is the matter of quality. Unless you are a Wizard of Woodworking, you're probably not going to be able to build a fine piece of furniture. Even if you have the skill and patience, the machinery and tools—not to mention the access to premium and exotic types of wood—are just not feasible for the amateur. (And if you weren't planning on working with wood, it's even worse: Most people don't have metal stamping presses or plastic injection molding machines in their basement.)

Buying allows you to match your storage pieces precisely with the rest of the furniture and decor in your baby's room. A contemporary book shelf is one thing, but a Victo-

rian version is something entirely different. The flexibility you get in buying just can't be beat if you have strong preferences in design.

You can probably figure out the rest of the reasons why buying is nice: Just remember the splinters and bandages, the paint stains on the floor and the assorted death threats you made during your last do-it-yourself project. Then contrast that with the thought of going to the store this afternoon and having a completed unit assembled and ready to go tonight.

Can you buy a toy chest, but build the shelves for inside your nursery closet? Or buy an antique pine cabinet but build new storage bins inside it? You bet: building or buying is not an either/or situation. Building and buying has a real nice ring to it and it's a solution you should consider when it comes to planning storage space.

Courtesy Noel-Joanna, Inc.

Courtesy Clarson International

# Storage Ideas
## The Basics

Before you run out and buy or build that storage piece, try to figure out exactly what it is you'll be storing. In your bedroom, you have sports coats, slacks, and silk blouses. Your hutch downstairs contains tableclothes and serving pieces. And the shelves in the den hold your CD player, a VCR, and the latest Stephen King best-seller.

Now, welcome to your baby's room. The closet contains 10-inch long t-shirts, booties that can fit in your hand, and snowsuits not big enough for your pet dog. The shelves hold more animals, stuffed that is, than Noah had to deal with, a fleet of toy trucks to

make General Motors jealous, and enough stacking, building, and connecting toys to keep the most curious builder busy for years.

Your baby, simply, has far different storage needs than you do. That's why what works in your bedroom sometimes won't work in hers. Other ideas can be adapted for the nursery with a little ingenuity. And yes, some storage solutions work no matter what room they're in. Who knows, you may even pick up an idea you can use for another room in the house.

## Baby's Closet

The first place to start is with the baby's closet. If you don't have a closet in the nursery, don't skip this section: you'll

probably get one by the time you figure out all the things you'll need to put in one.

The first thing you should probably do with the existing closet in the room is to gut it. Get rid of the pole, the shelf and anything else cluttering up the inside. Closet design has come a long way since your house was built and even if it's new, chances are, it's still not right for a baby. Baby's clothes, you see, are smaller than adult's. Poles and such designed for your clothing also create an enormous amount of wasted space because you can't double-rack clothing.

Fortunately, the design solution for your closet is probably sitting in a box in your local hardware, housewares, or department store. Vinyl-covered

wire rack systems, known as closet organizers, are one of this decade's greatest inventions and rather than give you complicated formulas to follow or intricate measurements to take to buy individual pieces, the best advice I can provide is to tell you to buy one of these kits.

These pre-fab kits, which are also offered in specialized children's versions, provide for multiple racks to hang clothes, shelving for storing folded clothing, and room for toys, hats, shoes, bags, and even those big boxes of disposable diapers. You can add matching wire rack baskets that slide out on tracks and come in two, three, and five-drawer sizes to store socks, dolls, blocks, and other toys.

If your closet is especially roomy, consider moving a small dresser or night stand in there. It will open up floor space in the room while organizing as many storage functions as possible in one centralized location in the room. Don't forget the inside of the door, either. It's a great spot for hooks, pegs, or even slim wire storage pieces that might hold books or assorted odds and ends.

There are even independent closet consultants who will come in and design a customized structure tailored for your use. That's a nice service, but the pre-fab kits make it a luxury you really don't need unless your closet problems are really serious. The kits are inexpensive, easy to install, and quite trim looking.

# Up Against the Walls

The simplest and sometimes cleanest answer to baby room storage is the open bookshelf unit. It can be free-standing, like a piece of furniture, or secured to the wall. It can have fixed or adjustable shelving. It can be in stained wood or finished laminate. It can be a trim four-by-six foot piece or it can cover an entire wall.

When considering open shelving for a nursery, follow the same rules for sturdiness, quality of finish, and flexibility that you would for any other room. Shelves should be at about twelve inches (thirty centimeters) deep: any more shallow and you'll find many things won't fit comfortably and any deeper and tiny arms won't be able to reach the back of the shelf. Figure about nine to ten inches (twenty-two to twenty-four centimeters) in height between shelves, although you might want a bit more for the large-scaled toys and stuffed ani-

mals kids tend to gather.

Closed door storage units call for the same dimensions, but watch the hinges and hardware for sharp edges and mechanisms that might pinch small fingers. Storage pieces with doors and closed fronts allow you to shut off the clutter, which is nice, but they also provide one more hinderance for a child learning to pick up after himself. A nice bonus though is that you can keep some items handy in a nursery, such as medicines or

*Facing page:* **Open shelving probably works best in a nursery, allowing for a great deal of flexibility and little potentially dangerous hardware.**

*Right:* **Storage bins—stationary or on wheels—make great catch-alls and are perfect for little ones trying to keep things neat. Bright colors can really liven up the decor, too.**

Courtesy Heller

scissors, in the locked drawer of a wall unit whereas an open shelf doesn't provide that kind of security.

A good compromise is a wall unit with both open and closed storage. Whatever you choose, keep in mind the height of who'll be using it: Shelving that starts halfway up the wall may look nice, but you—not your child—will be putting stuff away on those shelves for a lot of years until your child is old enough to reach them.

You may also wish to compartmentalize shelves with small upright dividers at various lengths. This creates a more orderly system for storing things, making a place for each possession. It works especially nice with balls and other round objects that won't stay still on long, flat shelves.

In short, you can't go wrong with shelving, open or closed, built-in or freestanding. But remember to position those storage units in logical

places. The shelf where you keep the diapers is going to be much more practical if it's next to the changing table. Clothing storage works best when it's placed near the closet. And arranging all toy storage devices on one side of the room makes for a neater layout, one that you hope your new little messmaker will learn faster than if storage were scattered about the room.

## Especially for Baby

Shelves are nice, but how about bins? Plastic bins in various colors and sizes, arranged neatly on a closet floor or on an open shelf provide the kind of storage space that's just right for babies about to become small children. A collection of bins, in assorted sizes, can be used to stow odd-shaped pieces that would get lost in big drawers or look disorganized on open shelving.

Bins are also a neat temporary solution if you're adapting an existing bookcase or

wall unit to the nursery. They can be used for a few years and then discarded or even reused someplace else when your piece returns to normal service. And by choosing brightly colored bins, you've added some visual interest to a sedate oak or teak wall unit.

Bins also represent a fine compromise in a great dilemma of parenting: trying to maintain a neat nursery while giving your child ready access to her possessions. Bins do that and more; they make it easy for kids to learn how to put those possessions away, too. Drawers and high shelves may be too complex, but tossing things in a bin is a concept that's easy to grasp.

Where do you get these bins? Only a few companies specifically market their products for use in children's rooms, but don't let that stop you. Big Tupperware pieces work great. So do adult plastic sweater, shoe, and clothing storage bins, and some of them even have tops. Head

for the housewares department and you'll find lots of Rubbermaid products and similar items that will do the trick. Use your imagination: A small plastic garbage can will perform miracles when it comes to stowing things. And don't forget the good old milk crate, in plastic or original wood. Since there aren't too many people still getting home delivery of dairy products, today's milk crate is more likely to be found in a store than on a doorstep, but it still makes a great storage unit.

Pegs are another device you might not have thought about too much, but they're also a clever idea for storage. Sooner or later you're going to get tired of using the closet to store things that are being used all the time. And if you don't, your child will. Pegs can hold clothes, as well as hats, stuffed animals, toys, and all sorts of things. You can even hang laundry bag sacks from pegs and store more things that way. Place a single peg on a short wall, line-up a row of them on a railing, or go to town and cover an entire wall in the nursery completely with pegboard to satisfy every storage need. Again, it's a matter of thinking differently for your baby's room than you would for yours.

Pegs and hooks aren't the only things you can hang around the nursery. Think of baskets as hanging bins. Bicycle baskets, flower baskets, even plastic bins all work nicely when converted to baby room storage. Just don't

forget to hang them at a height that everyone—you and your child—can use.

Hanging baskets, suspended from the ceiling, also make an imaginative storage device, especially if you decorate them like a balloon. Of course, you'll want to establish the ground rules with your toddler about hanging from the basket or overloading it. You can always play it safe by putting the basket on a pulley system that can be hoisted up out of harm's way whenever necessary.

Some storage alternatives take a traditional idea, such as conventional shelving, but add a new twist, such as a wall unit made of giant Tinkertoys, the oversized construction set. It's colorful, creative, and it certainly has "baby" written all over it. Best of all, you can rebuild it as your needs change or even change it back into a non-storage toy as your child gets older. The same idea works for other building and construction toys which you can find at your local toy store. You may find

Courtesy Community Playthings, Rifton, NY

Grown-ups tend to think of drawers when it comes to stowing things, but there are much better solutions for the baby's room. Hooks and pegs—set at baby's height—actually encourage clean ups, while bins and storage boxes (hide them behind doors if the clutter gets to you) are better suited to little hands and big objects.

Courtesy The Little Tikes Company

the cost very attractive and the effect quite pleasing. If you haven't seen the newer construction toys on the market, you owe it to you and your baby to see what's available before you buy just another wood-grained bookcase.

And what would a baby's room be without a toy chest? If there's any one product that seems perfect for a kid, it's a toy chest just like you had when you were a kid. Well, almost like the one you had. The toy chests many of us had growing up had two very seri-

ous design flaws that make them strictly taboo for use today. The first and most obvious had to do with the hinge that held up the lid or chest top. Those lids were not made to hold very much weight, so that when a child pushed on it or used it for support getting in or out of the chest, the results were sometimes fatal. Today toy chests are required to use a spring-loaded lid support that will hold the lid open in any position.

The second, less obvious, hazard of using older toy

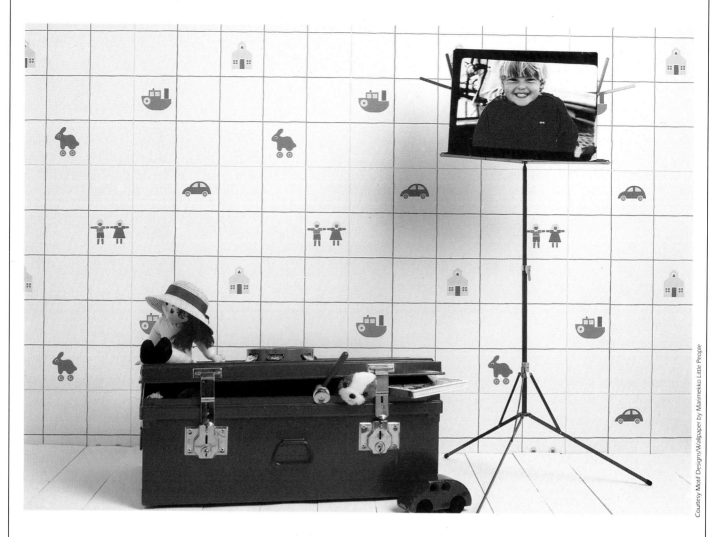

Courtesy Motif Designs/Wallpaper by Marimekko Little People

chests involved suffocation, due to inadequate ventilation of the toy box. Many children love to use their chest as a fort or other imaginary building, so today's products have ventilation holes or spaces between surfaces. Make sure you don't cover them up when you place a toy chest next to a wall.

Those new chests specifically manufactured to hold toys will meet all current safety standards, but old chests may not. Check the hinges and either replace them or get another chest. You can drill ventilation holes in an old toy box if needed. If it's a pre-1978 piece, it may contain leaded paint, so check it out thoroughly. The same goes for storage pieces that make great toy boxes but initially served another purpose. The most common is the old steamer trunk or footlocker. It's just right in size and shape for a toy box, but check the hinges and the ventilation. When in doubt, remove the top all together and you've got a real conversation piece.

## Slightly "Off-the-Wall"

One of the nice things about home furnishings these days is that great decorating ideas are coming from many different sources. The high-tech industrial look was imported from the factory. Clean, stark minimalism is really an off-shoot from offices and office buildings. Even ideas that were once thought of as being suitable only for a particular room, such as the kitchen, are now being applied for other functions as well. So let your imagination run wild.

You might run into vinyl-sheathed metal shelving, once a purely industrial product now being applied to homes. This type of shelving is turning up in closets all over the house, but there are some freestanding units that make for great storage in the nursery. And the bright, vibrant colors are perfect for baby's design schemes. Metal, locker-room-type enclosures are also catching on in the home and seem especially suited for the athletic baby, or at least the one who's going to be an athlete in his or her parent's eyes. Again, the colors are super and even a tough two-year-old isn't going to destroy a steel wall.

From the backyard comes the hammock. String one, or at least a piece of strong netting shaped like one, in the corner of your nursery. Or place a hammock between two parallel walls. It's a great catch-all for plush toys and even some clothes.

From the dining room, consider the plate shelf. Many old homes feature a narrow shelf surrounding the room only a foot or two beneath the ceiling. Sure, it's not exactly the most accessible space in the room, but as a place for toys your baby is not yet ready to play with—a toy shelf makes a great design accent.

The good old reliable clothes tree makes a welcome addition to any nursery, as well. It's a handy place for hanging up clothing used everyday, and many toys and stuffed animals come with hooks, so a tree could serve double duty as a toy storage device as well.

There are all kinds of ideas that will lend themselves to baby rooms. Keep your eyes open and your creativity cooking and who knows what great storage idea you'll come up with.

Don't get locked into the conventional when planning the storage spaces for your baby's room. Old footlockers or steamer trunks—properly updated to meet current safety standards—can be special toy chests and will work well beyond "ma-ma and da-da" days. "Costumers," what adults call clothes trees, make great, functional corner accessories. Speaking of corners, a hammocklike net can be fitted into a corner as storage for plush toys and dolls.

## A STEP-BY-STEP GUIDE
# How to Build a Themed Wall Shelf Unit

You'll need plenty of storage in your new baby's room, so every extra shelf helps. What's especially nice is a signature piece, a focal point for the room. Here are two ideas that you can build yourself, choosing the theme that best suits your new family member. And while the triplane may be considered a ''boy'' theme and the doll house a ''girl'' design, don't be hemmed in by stereotypes. Go with what you like.

1" × 12"

2'

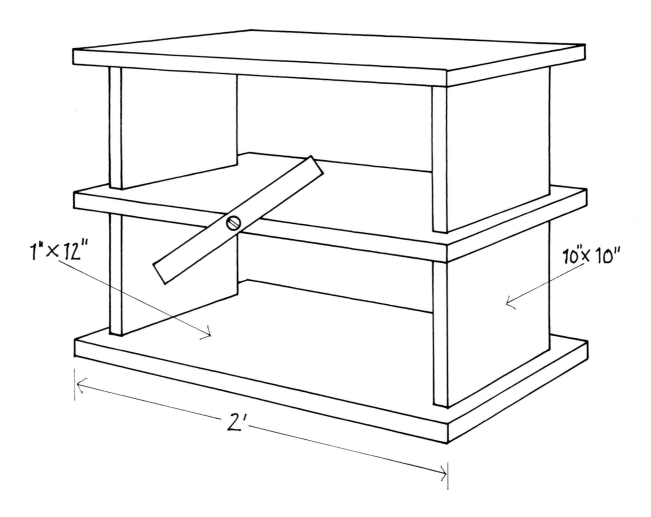

1" × 12"

10" × 10"

2'

**1.** For both designs, start with three pieces of finish grade 1-by-12-inch (2.5-by-30-centimeters) lumber, 2 feet (60 centimeters) long.

**2.** For the triplane, space these three boards parallel, 10 inches (25 centimeters) apart, using a 1-inch (2.54 centimeter) square piece of wood between each shelf (four pieces in total), nailed to the shelves 1 inch (2.54 centimeters) in from each end.

**3.** For the doll house, space the boards the same way, but use pieces of 1-by-12-inch (2.5-by-30-centimeter) board for the sides, nailed to the edge of the shelves. The doll house will also require one additional piece of 1-by-12-inch (2.5-by-30-centimeter) board, 28 inches (70 centimeters) long. Cut this board in half, using a mitre box, at a 45

degree angle. These two pieces will be the roof of the doll house, secured to the top shelf with nails. You can use an additional piece of 1 by 12 to support the roof, placing it midway on the top shelf.

**4.** For the triplane, cut a piece of 1-inch (2.5-centimeter) square wood about four inches (10 centimeters) long for the propeller, placing it midway on the middle shelf, or, for a real nice touch, go to a local hobby shop and buy a propeller from a gas-powered, radio-controlled airplane.

**5.** Paint your triplane or doll house according to your own tastes. You could make the airplane a re-creation of the Red Baron himself. Your doll house can be a mini-Tara. Go to a toy store and see how similar items are finished.

**6.** When your new wall unit is completed, attach it to the wall using three L-shaped shelf brackets available in any hardware store. If the unit will be used mostly by your child, place it about one-third of the way up the wall. If you're going to place mostly "look-but-don't-touch" collectibles on these shelves, place it higher on the wall.

**7.** As options, you can paint the wall behind the shelves to add to the effect, or place fabric behind it to give a coordinated look. You could also use cork-board, or even a thin piece of plywood. You may also want to place pegs along the edge of the lowest shelf for hanging things, or pegs on the slope of the roof of the doll house to use for holding hats.

When you're done, you'll have a themed "fantasy" wall unit that will be a real attention-getter.

**CHAPTER 4**

# The Finishing Touches

N ow, it's time to really kick into high gear and add the finishing touches, the elements that will make your nursery a great place for both your baby and you. And there's a lot involved in it. Yes, you've done the major work, painting and decorating, selecting, and sometimes even building the furniture for your baby's room, but a nursery is more than just a fresh coat of paint and some new furniture. All the things that make a difference in your world—lighting, music, temperature, pictures, and home security—are also significant in your baby's world. That's why getting all these little details right is just as important as the nursery basics. So, let's take a look around this new room and see what's still needed.

# Lighting Up a Baby's World

The first thing you'll notice when you walk into your nursery is either total darkness because there's no lighting in the room or, almost as bad, too much light from a bright, cold, and glaring ceiling fixture.

There are two ways to approach lighting any room, the baby's included. The first is permanent light fixtures, such as a ceiling light or wall sconce. The second is the portable lamp, usually either a table-top or floor-mounted design. Each has its advantages and together they can do wonders.

If you have a ceiling light, keep it. You may want to take a look at the overhead fixture, however. Remember that the new occupant of this room is going to be spending a fair amount of time on her back looking up at the ceiling. A functional but smart-looking fixture will do just fine.

Where you may need to make a switch is in the switch. Chances are, you have a wall-mounted on/off switch. It's a good idea to replace that with a soft-touch dimmer switch, where a rheostat lets you control the intensity of the light. Get one that also has a fast push on/off switch as well. It allows you to keep the level of light set at one point whereas a switch without this feature forces you to dial up your light level with every use.

The dimmer, of course, lets you create various light settings depending on the mood and time of day. Most lighting authorities recommend a 150 to 200 watt bulb for an average size room and with the rheostat you'll be able to control that lighting at an infinite number of levels. Go full light for play time and changing diapers, medium light for feeding, and soft lighting for naps and quiet times. Even if you're not handy with electricity, wall switches are extremely easy to install—just remember to shut off the power from the main circuit breakers or fuses whenever you're doing electrical work.

By the way, if you don't have a wall switch and your celing fixture is controlled by a pull chain, don't despair. Put in a three-way-socket—again a relatively easy do-it-yourself electrical task. Using a three-way bulb (try a 50/150 watt), you'll get almost the same effect, although you won't have the infinite settings.

Even if you have a ceiling fixture, it's a good idea to also consider a portable light for your baby's room. Sometimes an overhead light is just too harsh no matter how much you dim it and there are times, such as when you're reading a bedtime story or checking

Lighting is an important element in your new baby's room. A night-light, either one that plugs into an outlet or one built into a nursery lamp, is a must. In addition to night-light settings, some lamps have music boxes or moving scenes; others will coordinate with crib bedding or wall coverings.

Courtesy Judi's Originals

your baby to see how his diaper rash is doing, when you'll want a more directed light source.

Lamps designed especially for the nursery come in all shapes and sizes. Many feature favorite characters, from generic lambs and teddy bears to Mickey Mouse, Big Bird, and Snoopy. Of course, when you buy any product for your baby that features a recognizable face or figure on it, remember that she doesn't care who the character is: She doesn't know the difference between Disney and Dizzy Gillespie and couldn't care less whether that's the official version of a product or a reasonable facsimile. Go for the design, colors, and quality that look best to you and worry about the characters later. She'll be watching *Sesame Street* soon enough as it is.

Many of the nursery lamps

also contain a few nice extras. Most have a built-in night-light setting, which you'll find especially helpful when you want to take a quick peek into the crib late at night. Some feature music boxes, which play a tune or two when wound up. That's nice, but keep in mind your mobile, or perhaps a stuffed animal or two might already have a music box inside. While having assorted songs to lull your baby to sleep keeps her from getting tired of one tune, you may be paying for a redundant feature you just don't need.

The same goes for nursery lamps with moving parts. Some have a turning carousel or spinning figurines. Will your baby really be able to see these actions from inside his crib? Probably not, if you've positioned your lamp correctly. (More on that in a minute.) So, get a lamp with a night-light, but forget about the other doodads.

Now, just where should you put that lamp? The top of a chest is usually the best spot, away from your baby's reach, but near the crib or rocking chair. Remember to watch the lamp cord when baby becomes mobile. Because some poorly positioned table lamps can create problems for toddlers who like to reach out and touch everything, some people use floor lamps instead. That may solve some problems, but you still have to watch grabby little hands. In any case, floor lamps are an alternative if you don't have any proper horizontal surfaces in the nursery.

A second alternative is the wall lamp. Sconces, which are just wall-mounted fixtures, are staging something of a comeback these days, but their sophisticated, modern design may not be suitable for a nursery. Sway lamps, which are portable-type fixtures suspended from the ceiling, are another way to go, although at the moment, they're not especially in style. At the end of this chapter is a do-it-yourself wall lamp that just might light up your life—and your baby's—in the right way.

You'll notice I haven't talked about fluorescent lighting yet. No matter what the advantages of these types of bulbs— they deliver three times as much lighting as incandescents for the same wattage, plus they last 20 times longer than regular bulbs—most people still can't get used to them

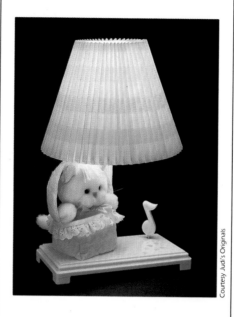

Courtesy Judi's Originals

*Above and right:* **Music, music everywhere: that about sums up the nearly endless possibilities for sound in the nursery. Music boxes have been around for centuries, but today's baby can select from a veritable juke box of sounds. The latest choice on the market are mobiles with built-in cassette players, so you can be the disk jockey.**

for bedrooms. If you feel differently, check into all-in-one fixtures that need no special wiring as a lighting source to shine over changing tables or set into wall unit shelving.

And of course, no matter what electrical device you're buying, always look for the U.L. listing. That means an independent testing source, Underwriter's Laboratory, has checked out the product and it's safe to use. Don't you wish everything in life was as easy as that?

# A Little Night Music

I suppose the fine art of lullaby singing is still alive and well, but for those who can't carry a tune, thank heavens for the music box. In mechanical form, music boxes have been around for centuries, and while they may have been upstaged more recently by electronic devices, music boxes are still a welcome addition to any nursery.

Courtesy Fisher-Price

Courtesy Judi's Originals

*Left and below:* Not every sound for baby is music to your ears. Devices that recreate the sounds of mother's womb are offered in many forms, from teddy bears to the inside of the crib bedding. You can also try prerecorded audio tapes which, naturally, have been dubbed womb tunes.

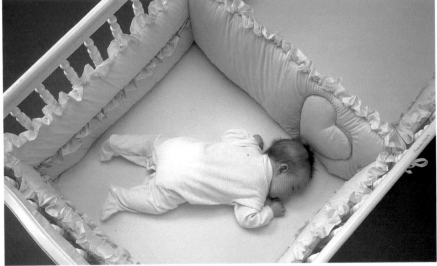

Courtesy Judi's Originals

Consider all the sources of songs in today's nursery: First, as mentioned earlier, is the nursery lamp with music box. Many stuffed animals also feature windup music mechanisms. Mobiles for cribs usually have the ability to play a tune or two, as do some other crib attachment toys. There are freestanding music boxes, with and without moving figures, and a whole host of infant toys that play music.

Your baby would never know a quiet moment if you

had them all in her room. Music boxes are nice, so we recommend you get one or two, but choose them carefully. One should be in a mobile, close to baby and playing a familiar tune every night. A second source of music should be more portable, perhaps in a stuffed animal so that it travels with your baby, providing a reassuring sound wherever she is. Unless you're planning on your baby being a concert virtuoso (or a disk jockey), we think that should be enough.

But just as you've progressed in your listening habits, so should the nursery. That's why a tape recorder especially for the nursery is a great idea. You can create your own tapes of favorite lullabies or buy some of the prerecorded versions now coming onto the market. Also available are bedtime stories, nursery rhymes, and assorted tales, all of which can make for great nursery listening.

There are now cassette players especially marketed for

the nursery, but any self-contained portable unit with built-in speaker will do. Battery operated units have the extra advantage of not having a power cord. In a few years, I predict, the tape player is going to be as commonplace in baby's room as the lamp.

There are also products, both freestanding units and prerecorded tapes, starting to come on the market that simulate the sound of the mother's womb. Before you start laughing—or maybe after you're finished—stop and think about it. There's been some research done that shows a newborn feels more secure when it hears the sound—something akin to light waves and a muted heartbeat. Stranger things have turned out to be true, so consider womb sounds, either on tapes or from a heart-shaped device that fits in the crib. You may even want to give it a try yourself some night when you're having trouble falling asleep.

# The Electronic Baby

When our parents and grandparents wanted to check on us in our cribs in the middle of the night, there was only one way to do it: get up, come out of bed or from the living room sofa during a TV commercial, tiptoe into the nursery, take a look around, and then breathe a sigh of relief that everything was just fine.

Then a few years ago, a product came along that changed everything, and in doing so, created a whole new category of virtual necessities for the nursery: baby monitoring devices. Using the technology of intercoms, several companies now make baby monitors that allow you to eavesdrop on your baby.

The monitors come in several varieties, but they all work essentially the same way: A transmitting unit is placed in the nursery, which sends signals to a receiver that can be placed in your bedroom or even clipped on to your belt if you're moving around the house. Some monitors just detect sound and it's up to you to figure out if it's your baby crying or just the window shade blowing in the wind. Better monitors allow you to actually hear what's going on in the room, much like a one-way walkie-talkie. Deluxe models are two-way systems, meaning that you can talk back to your baby, soothing her from afar and perhaps saving you a trip, or at least telling

Courtesy Playskool Baby, Inc

**Perhaps the most important—not to mention the most useful—electronic device to come along for the baby's room is the nursery monitor. Essentially, it works like an intercom, allowing you to eavesdrop on the nursery from the living room. Of course, the monitor is no substitute for personal parental monitoring, but it is a must for just about every home with a baby.**

her you're on your way. These monitors are usually freestanding devices and either have a nursery look or a high-tech appearance. A new twist on the whole idea is a nursery lamp with a built-in monitor, which can cut down on the chest-top clutter. Generally, the transmitting unit plugs into your household current, while the receiver is battery operated.

Nursery monitors are a great invention and unless you live in a studio apartment, you should consider a monitor an absolute necessity. Of course, electronic devices will never be a complete substitute for personal attention, but they sure make this baby business a lot easier.

With the success of monitors has come a whole parade of electronic monitoring devices. One is a door alarm in case Junior decides to toddle out of the nursery on his own one night. Another is a mat you place in front of the crib that alerts you to a possible escape attempt. Still others work lights, dimming them automatically on a timer. And by the time you read this there will no doubt be even more similar products on your store's shelves.

In fact the latest, and perhaps the ultimate, monitoring device is a system that Sony has been trying out: It's a tripod-mounted Camcorder camera that relays a video picture to a monitor in your living room. Of course, you can use the components for regular video purposes later on, but I think this may be taking the Big Brother idea a little too far. And talk about keeping things on budget!

It's up to you to separate the useful from the useless. If you're the busy type, or just get too involved in what you're doing and tend to tune out the world around you, some of these devices are going to be very helpful. But if you're the type who is always checking on your baby, or have a small apartment, your money may be better spent elsewhere.

One other electronic product, however, rates as an absolute necessity: the smoke alarm. In fact, your home should have at least one, whether you have a newborn or not. This product, which lets out a shrill alarm when it detects the presence of smoke and toxic gasses in the air, is a great life saver and one of the few bargains of home security: prices have dropped to under ten dollars over the past few years.

Your smoke detector does not have to be in the baby's room itself. Position one on the ceiling in a hall leading to bedrooms or at the top of a flight of stairs. Some units work on batteries, others on household electricity: Either is okay, but it is recommended that if using a non-battery model, you wire it directly into your home's electric service rather than plugging it into an outlet, where it can be unplugged by a child or accidently shut off by a light switch. Battery-operated units should be checked every month or so, although many models have warning devices—they often sound like a bird chirping—that tell you your battery is wearing down.

While we're on the subject of safety devices, don't forget to make sure your medicine cabinet is fully stocked with first aid items: You may even want to consider a separate first aid kit just for the nursery. Keep it near the changing table or attached to the inside of the closet door.

There are some great inventions and products out there that will make your life easier (and longer). All you have to do is use them.

# Weathering Heights

When you're cold, you can turn up the heat, and when it's too warm to sleep at night, you can always pop on the air conditioner. Your baby doesn't have it as lucky. So, it's always a good idea to take special care to make sure you're adequately safeguarding another part of her new environment: the temperature and indoor climate.

The first step is to install a small thermometer for your baby's room. A little hand-held or wall-mounted mercury thermometer will do the job just fine. It's a minor point, but you'll be able to accurately gauge how hot or cold the room is, whether you're in your pajamas at three in the morning or your winter coat at three in the afternoon.

You've probably picked a nice, snug warm room for the nursery, but if that's not the case—or it's a little too warm and snug—it's time to consider some remedies. In heaters you of course want to consider devices that have no exposed heating elements and are cool to the touch. Some of the oil-filled, sealed units now on the market fit the bill, although they warm the room gradually rather than throwing off a great gust of hot air, which is probably just as well. You don't want a lot of air— hot or cold—blowing directly on baby.

Just as obviously, electric fans are out of the question for nurseries. The danger is just too great. Window air conditioners with fan settings are the best choices for those hot summer days and nights, but again, watch the output of the appliance in relation to the position of the crib.

One device that might solve both heating and cooling

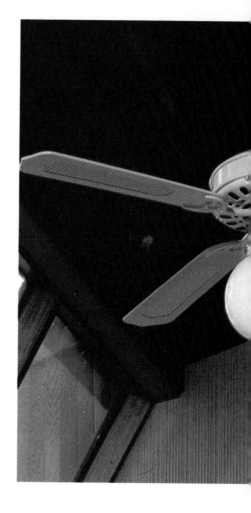

problems—and one that represents no safety problem whatsoever—is the reversible ceiling fan. Once only associated with Casablanca or sleepy Southern towns, ceiling fans have proven to be efficient, safe, and inexpensive sources of temperature control. With the blades spinning one way in hot weather, hot air is forced up from the lower levels of the room and dissipated. Rotating the other way in winter, the heat that gathers near the ceiling is pushed back down to where you are. Fans are quiet— compared to air conditioners and even portable floor and table fans—and out of reach. That's what makes them good

*Left:* The ceiling fan, long thought of as an accessory used only in tropical climates, is a good way to cool off your baby's room. Unlike an air conditioner, it will not blow a direct stream of air on your baby, and is much safer than a portable fan. A ceiling fan is also useful in the winter as it helps to circulate warm air throughout your baby's room.

Courtesy American Olean Tile Co.

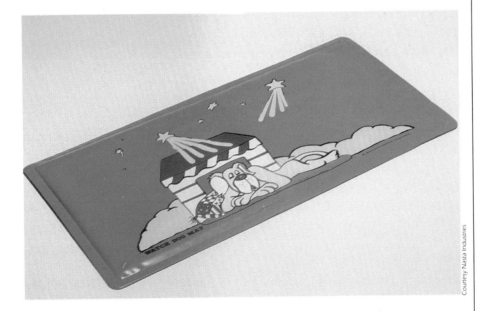

*Above:* Today, there are all sorts of electronic devices on the market to protect your baby and warn you if he attempts a midnight escape. This mat, which you place in front of a crib, does the trick quite nicely.

for your baby's room.

Make sure you get a fan with a reversible motor—most have that feature today—and also look for one with at least three speeds. They either work on a pull chain or can be controlled by a wall switch. Many even have built-in lights, an extra nice touch especially when the fan replaces an existing overhead fixture.

One other aspect of your baby's climatic environment needs to be watched and that's humidity. With the advent of the ultrasonic humidifier, that becomes a very easy thing to do. I'm going to assume that lack of humidity—not enough moisture in the air, usually caused by heating systems that dry out the air—is the problem, rather than too much humidity. (There are appliances available to take moisture out of the air, but this is usually a problem only in basements and I hope you haven't put the nursery in the basement.)

Ultrasonic humidifiers are about the size of a portable tape player/radio and can convert about a gallon of tap water into twelve hours of humidifying vapor. The old belt-driven humidifiers are simply ineffective in comparison with these new appliances. They're quiet, easy to keep clean, and one fill-up lasts all night. If your house—and your baby's room—is dry, a humidifier is a quick, easy solution.

Everybody always complains about the weather, but now you can do something about it.

Courtesy Nasta Industries

Courtesy Gerber Furniture Group, Century Products, Inc.

The total nursery ensemble look can make anyone a decorating genius thanks to coordinated merchandise, ranging from basic bedding to dust ruffles to mobile to lamp shade to rug. **Don't forget the most important rule of the coordinated nursery: If you dress your baby in the same fabric as the room, finding her may be quite a difficult task.**

# The Soft Touch

So far, most of what you've bought, borrowed, built, and maybe even begged for, qualifies under the heading of hard goods: metal, wood, and plastic furniture, furnishings, and devices. But one of the real joys of putting the finishing touches on a nursery these days is picking out the bedding and coordinated accessories that are the icing on the cake. Today, your choices are incredibly wide and varied when it comes to a baby comforter and sheets.

In the old days, your choice would have been a blue quilt with an elephant knitted on or a pink quilt with a lamb embroidery. Sheets would have run the gamut from white to white . . . and "everything" in between. The new variety available is a welcome choice. You say you'd like a Victorian nursery with soft white eyelet bedding and plenty of ruffles? You've got it. Or you'd like a bright, bold design in primary blues and reds? No problem. Maybe a muted collection of pastel colors stitched together in a quiltwork pattern is more

Courtesy Judi's Originals

to your liking.

The choices are endless and the selection goes far beyond just a crib comforter and coordinating sheets. Many nursery ensembles, as they're called, can include up to twenty matching items, from crib bumpers to lamps to diaper stackers to dust ruffles to switchplates to garbage cans to picture frames to wall hangings. Some companies have even contracted with outside sources to coordinate rugs and wallpaper with their bedding groups.

When buying bedding, ob-viously you would look for the same features as you would for your own sheets and blankets. Figure you'll need about six fitted crib sheets, two to three blankets, one comforter or quilt and a couple of pillow cases to get you started. The pillow itself should only be used for decoration when the baby isn't in residence: she doesn't need it for sleeping. In fact, the only real necessity out of all the coordinated accessories is a bumper, which acts as a cushion in the crib, cuts down on drafts, and generally helps to create a more secure and cozier spot for your newborn to get used to her new world.

A soft wall sculpture that coordinates with your crib bedding is a nice decorative element, especially if you're not that artistic and haven't painted anything special for the nursery. These wall hangings sometimes feature TV or movie characters like Mickey Mouse or Big Bird, but often they are just whimsical designs. Balloons are an especially popular theme, but horses, rainbows, and the ever-present teddy bear can also be seen.

More traditional framed pictures can also work nicely and you can probably pick out a print or painting that may have a longer lifespan than will the nursery designs that coordinate with crib bedding.

Coordination also extends to window treatments. Sometimes curtains are offered as part of a nursery ensemble, or maybe you've picked out a nice pattern that pulls the whole room together. If, however, curtains aren't offered with the ensemble, don't despair. It's easy to make curtains from panels cut from sheets that are part of the ensemble. Use curtain rods top and bottom to create a shirred effect for windows, French doors, or even a doorless closet. Make sure you do your measurements after the rods have been installed. For windows, measure within the frame, on the surface of the frame, or just attach the curtains directly to the window sash.

# Going Mobile

Often, you can purchase a crib mobile that matches your bedding as well, but mobiles are another product that run the gamut from cute characters to sophisticated patterns. Mobiles also happen to be the first of the many so-called "baby-minding" products you'll use. These are items that entertain and amuse your baby while you go off and do something foolhardy, like eat, catch your breath, or act grown-up for a few minutes.

It's a task mobiles are perfectly suited for. Attaching to the side rail of a crib, they offer the baby a panorama of shapes and colors to keep him busy for at least a few minutes anyway. Most mobiles also have a wind-up mechanism that rotates the figures and sometimes plays music as well. Each is a nice add-on. Some mobiles have soft, sewn figures, others are made of plastic, and some are constructed of wood.

It all comes down to a matter of taste, but there are a few things to keep in mind, whatever style mobile you buy. Most mobiles on the market have figures that are essentially perpendicular to the baby. Think about lying on your back and looking up at the *bottoms* of all those cute bears and ducks and ponies. Obviously, this is not the way it's supposed to be. Your baby will only get the full effect when the figures are angled towards her point of view and that's a design you should

If you buy a crib mobile, you're entering the world of "baby-minders," neat little products that will keep your baby busy—for a few minutes anyway—while you take a breather from the parenting game. Mobiles, which sometimes also play music, do the job quite nicely. Remember that mobiles, like any activity toy you put on or in your crib, should be removed once your baby starts to push up on his hands or knees, at about five months of age.

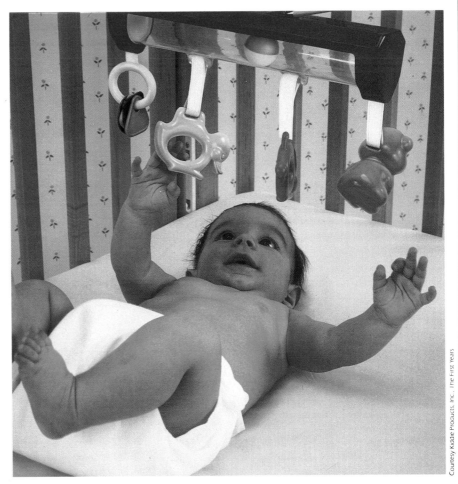

most certainly look for. One other nice option on some soft mobiles is that the individual figures are detachable and can be used as toys when your baby gets a little older. She'll probably have all the little stuffed animals she'll need, but a few more never hurt.

As with any product used in the crib, a mobile should be removed as soon as your baby can push up on her hands or knees, which is usually at about five months. This also goes for crib gyms or activity toys that are suspended across the crib or tied over one side. Once your baby can reach—and possibly pull down and become entangled in—these toys, it's time to get rid of them. The same kinds of rules, in fact, pertain to all of your baby's first toys. Once she starts moving about the crib, all those lovely stuffed animals and such make great stepping stones for daring escapes. Take them all out of the crib and let your baby play with her new toys under close supervision.

Rattles, teethers, and pacifiers are other toy-type devices you and your baby will be using fairly early on. Keep in mind a couple of common-sense rules when dealing with these products:

• Never tie a pacifier or rattle to a piece of string or ribbon long enough to wrap around your baby's neck. To be on the safe side, avoid strings on any product for your baby.

• Watch all products for small parts. Generally, anything less than two inches (five centimeters) in diameter should be avoided as smaller objects can get lodged in the back of your baby's mouth or throat. If you can pull any small pieces off, don't use the product.

• Take these small objects out of the crib when baby is sleeping just to be extra careful.

• Above all, if you're unsure about a product's size, construction, or content, just don't use it. That's the best rule.

79

# Potpourri

Your baby's room is just about complete. But here are a few more ideas of interest that you just might be able to work into your decorating scheme.

You can achieve a different look for your nursery by using painted backgrounds for furniture in the room. Paint a skyline behind a chest to give it extra height and depth. Or paint a canopy on the wall behind—and even the ceiling above—your crib. You can even take the triplane wall shelf from Chapter Three and have a trail of exhaust smoke coming out from behind it, across the wall and onto the ceiling.

The same effect can be had with a single sheet of plywood cut out to resemble a castle, a forest of trees, or even a crescent moon. These can be painted and tacked up behind cribs, dressers, and other furniture to add an extra dimension to your baby's room.

If, no matter how hard you try, there's still a cluttered corner of the room full of baby stuff that refuses to get neat, try a large, folding screen that sections off the room. Freestanding screens aren't tough to make: just stretch some fabric over a plywood frame and use door or cabinet hinges to hold the panels together.

If the *totally* coordinated look is what you're after, you can buy extra sheets and cover *everything* with the same fabric. That means waste cans, lamp shades, doorknobs, switchplates, shelf liners, and picture frames. Just don't *ever* make your own baby clothes out of the same fabric—or you'll never be able to find your baby in the room.

Courtesy Lillian Vernon Corp.

**A STEP-BY-STEP GUIDE**
# How to Make Your Own Sun Light

Lighting that hangs on the wall of the nursery has the advantage of being portable, yet far away from grabbing hands and limited table top space. Here's a way to build one such wall lamp that might brighten up your nursery.

**1.** Cut out a 14-by-20-inch (35-by-50-centimeter) piece of plain white fabric and staple it to 6-inch (15-centimeter) wide framing strips around all four sides, creating a reverse shadow box effect.

**2.** Take a freestanding spotlight, such as a plant lamp and attach it to the *inside* of the top of the frame, either clamping it or screwing it into the frame, depending on the fixture you've selected. Point the light to the center of the framed area, making sure the bulb is at least 3 inches away from the fabric itself.

**3.** Cut a little notch in the lower corner of the frame, so that the electrical cord from the fixture can run down the wall and plug into a nearby outlet. If possible, secure the wire directly to the wall so it cannot be pulled away.

**4.** Take the portion of the cord that is outside the frame and attach a cord-mounted on/off switch at a convenient height. The instructions for securing the switch will be on the package. It is very easy to do.

**5.** Now, paint a picture of the sun on the fabric, making it whimsical with a big smiling face or more artistic, as your talent allows. Add clouds, a foreground, even the moon and airplanes if you're up for it.

You'll now have another work of art for your baby's room...and this one will light up the nursery to boot.

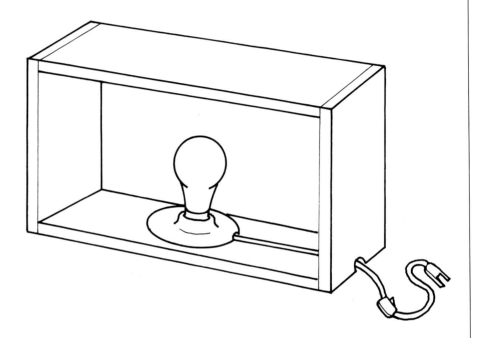

Illustrations: Kenneth Spengler

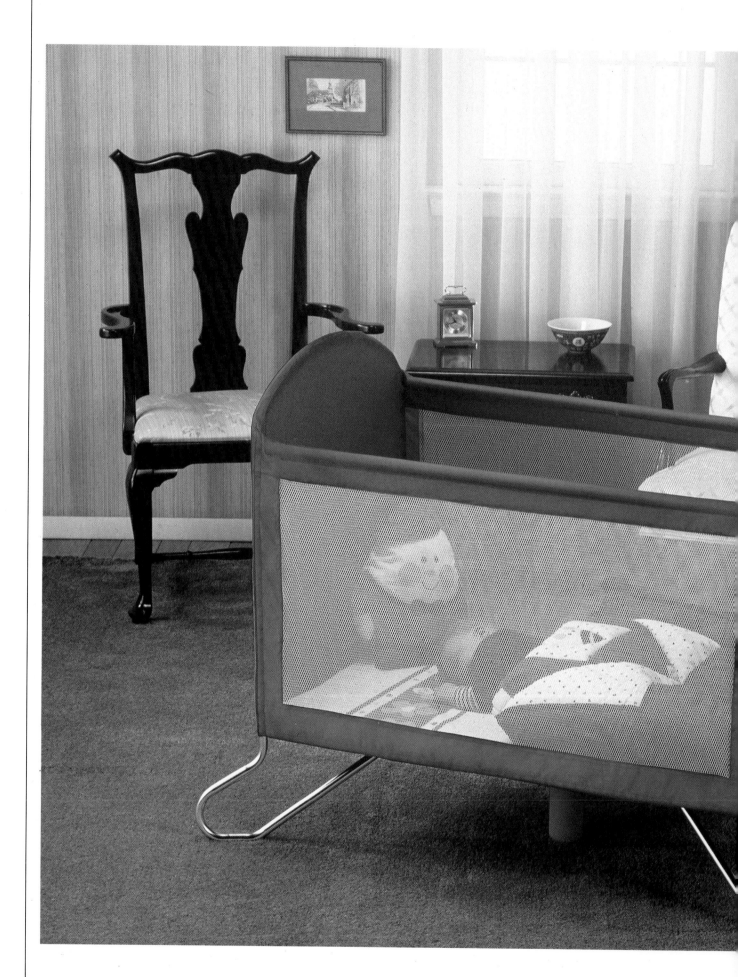

Courtesy Fisher-Price

## CHAPTER 5

# Other Rooms Of The House

U nless you live in a one-room shack— or today's modern equivalent, the studio or efficiency apartment—pretty soon you're going to figure out that perhaps this book has been incorrectly named. *Baby Rooms*, you're going to find, tend to be whatever room your baby is in. Because wherever your baby goes, he rarely travels alone. His crib may be in his room, but that won't do him a whole lot of good when you want him to take a nap in the living room. If you'll be spending a good part of your day in the kitchen and you want him to join you, he can't just pull up a kitchen chair and sip a cup of coffee at the breakfast table.

Babies need to be bathed, too, and that's a project for the bathroom, which opens up another roomful of possibilities. Then there's your bedroom, a brother or sister's bedroom, the den, and all the rooms, halls, and vestibules in between. Each requires specialized baby gear, safety-proofing, and precautionary measures to make them just right for your baby.

Baby's room, it appears, is more accurately baby's house.

So, exactly what do you need outside of your baby's room? What's the minimum amount of "stuff" required to make your baby comfortable, happy, and secure in the other rooms of your house? And what should you look for in these products?

First, you should know it's

Your baby's room, you'll soon find out, isn't confined to the nursery: it's wherever your baby is. When your baby starts venturing out into the rest of the house—to the kitchen, the bathroom, the living room, or perhaps an older brother or sister's room—you'll need a whole host of new devices to restrain, contain, and entertain. Portable playpens (*above*) that fold for easy storage are a popular choice and will accept many of the same items you use in the crib. Remember that when your baby is in her crib, away from you, it is important to have a nursery monitoring device (*right*).

not so bad. You can get by with just a few key products around the house. But you should also know that you'll probably end up buying many more products than you ever imagined. Many parents-to-be can't understand the logic behind certain products and devices, until the right time arrives and they need them. Then they wonder how they ever got along without them.

Many of these products qualify under the general heading of "baby-minders," devices that allow you to maintain some semblance of normal adult existence while providing a safe and sometimes entertaining environment. Almost all of these products also have an incredibly short lifespan . . . painfully short considering the prices of some of them. You'll be using some of these items for as short a period of time as five or six months. And unlike cribs that convert to beds and changing tables that become desks, there is nothing—absolutely nothing—that you can do with these products when you're finished with them. Of course, if you're planning on having ten or eleven kids the products will wear out long before you do. But short of that, these things won't even make good planters when your baby is done with them.

But when your hands are full with dinner or the telephone, when it's been a long day and you need a little time for yourself, or you just want the extra peace of mind that some of these products offer, they represent worthwhile investments. So, consider your space, patience, and budget limitations and see what's right—and important—for you and your new baby.

One other thing to consider as your baby starts to use other rooms in the house: The same safety inspection you made in the nursery has to be carried out for the rest of the house. Electrical outlets, doorknobs, cabinets, and drawers all have to be baby-proofed with the appropriate products (see pages 18 to 19 for more information). Sharp table corners have to be covered and low shelves of assorted knick-knacks and bric-a-brac (whatever that is) have to be cleared. Electric cords and appliances need to be properly stowed. It's time to get back down on your hands and knees to make sure everything checks out from a baby's-eye perspective. You might even find that lost earring you've been searching for.

Courtesy Playskool Baby, Inc.

# Baby in the Kitchen

The kitchen is the room you'll probably be spending the most amount of time in with your baby. This is where you'll be feeding her, where she'll be when you're eating, and also when you're fixing dinner or doing the breakfast dishes. But it's also the most potentially dangerous room in the house. There are plenty of electrical appliances here, from toasters to food processors, each one a potential hazard. Drawers, cabinets, and closets abound here and each is a place for baby to explore and get hurt in. Add in fire and heat from the stove and water from the sink and you have a very hazardous place for the little ones.

That's why some rules are especially necessary in the kitchen. You need to put locks and child-proof latches on every openable storage area in the room. Knives, plastic bags, matches, toxic substances—such as detergents and cleaning products—and glassware all have to be kept behind closed doors.

The stove is an especially dangerous place. Keep pots and pans on the back burners whenever possible with all handles turned sideways, rather than hanging over the front or outside. There are special safety devices designed specifically for kitchen ranges. One is a large plastic barrier that surrounds the stove, but allows you to reach over it.

Another creates a "cage" around the stove-top to prevent pots from falling over the side.

It is critical that you know that burns are one of the highest causes of severe injury and death to infants and young children. Even hot, steaming coffee (approximately 155°F [68°C]) causes a third degree burn to a young child in *one* second. Your best bet in the kitchen is to put your baby into a product that will contain her and keep her away from trouble spots. You can use an infant carrier seat, a high chair, a swing, a playpen, or a walker; although all will do the trick, chances are, you'll mostly be using one of the first three in the kitchen.

One of the first places outside of your arms your baby will be is in the infant carrier seat, a hard plastic shell you can use for feeding, napping, or quick trips around the house. One place you can't use them is in your car. Although they may look like car seats, carrier seats aren't built to the same rigid standards and won't protect your baby in case of trouble.

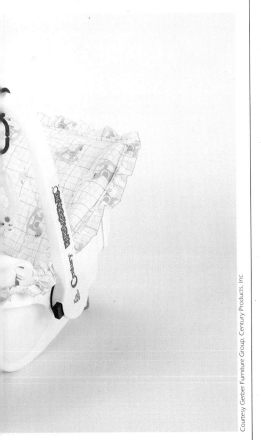

# Infant Carrier Seats

They are sometimes called carrier seats, sometimes infant seats, and sometimes baby carriers—or any combination thereof—but whatever the name, they are neat little products . . . and probably the first place outside of the nursery where your baby will be hanging out.

Essentially a hard plastic molded shell, covered in vinyl or fabric, and often sporting a movable handle, this product is more often than not used as a seat rather than as a carrier, for feeding, napping, or just as a convenient parking spot from which your baby can watch the world go by. In the carrier mode, they make solid transporters between house and car or even from room to room in the house. But for touring the local malls or a day

in the country, carrier seats really won't do the trick. They put all their weight on your arms, rather than your shoulders or some other part of your body better suited for loads. Pretty soon that little bundle of joy is going to be as much fun to carry around as last week's laundry.

One place never to use infant seats is in an automobile, as an infant car seat. Although in many cases they resemble infant car seats, baby carriers are made of lesser grades of plastic that aren't designed to hold up under impact. And the restraining belts you'll find in baby carriers aren't even close in function to car seat belts. They may look alike, but they aren't interchangeable.

Some infant carriers have a little compartment underneath for storing a diaper or two and perhaps a small bottle. It's a

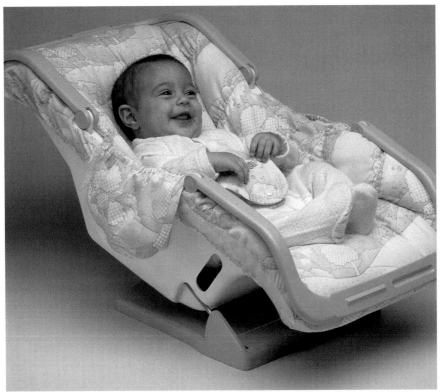

nice bonus and probably worth the extra dollar or two. Some carriers can also be used as the seats in baby swings, but they're generally sold as a set so you have to be ready to lay out the money for both products at the same time.

When shopping for a carrier seat, look for one with a wide, sturdy base for stability and a nonskid bottom surface. Check for the overall construction of the item, but again, don't expect them to be as rigid or well-built as car seats. If you're picking up a used infant carrier, there are no federal rules regulating the products and models built ten or more years ago are probably very similar to what's on the market today. If the seat pad has seen better days, you can pick up a new cover that slips over the seat easily. Watch for cracks or chipped plastic: Since carriers are not that expensive, it may pay to buy a new one if you find there are problems with used seats.

Once you start using your infant carrier seat, a few commonsense rules apply. The safety belt provided is there to be used: Even if your baby will only be in it for a few minutes, belt her in. This may be the day she learns to squirm. Seats can be placed on tabletops—that's one of their great advantages—but always position them far away from the edge of the table. Most injuries occur when suddenly active babies fall out of the seat or the entire carrier falls with your baby in it. Remember that infants can push off of

other objects with their feet and so move their carriers.

You'll want to move your baby out of the carrier once she starts really moving around and getting active, usually about five months of age. Many products will give more exact ages in their instructions. So, yes, this is one of those short-term baby-minders. But before she gets into a high chair—and before your left arm falls off from holding her during every feeding, consider an infant carrier seat as a practical alternative.

## High Chairs

Next to cribs and car seats, high chairs are probably the most often purchased product for babies. The reasons are pretty obvious. As an infant, your child can't sit up in a regular chair. As she gets older, she may be able to sit straight, but she'll still be too low to use your table as an eating surface. And even if she could, her eating habits (or lack of) and propensity for mixing the mashed potatoes with the chocolate milk may

make a separate tray for her a quite desirable feature.

Today's high chairs address all three of those criteria in smart fashion. Essentially, a metal or wooden frame holds a vinyl or cloth-covered seat scaled to baby's size. A built-in and removable tray keeps your baby's food away from your food, as well as the floor, the furniture, the dog, and with luck the walls.

You'll want to look for a high chair with good stability, which means a wide stance and solid construction. High chairs, too, come with safety straps, which should be used at all times. If you're going with a used high chair, check to make sure the straps are in good shape: If not, a local store may have a replacement, or you may contact the manufacturer directly. If you can't replace the safety belt, get another high chair. And remember that trays should not be considered substitutes for safety belts. An active child can easily slide out under the

Courtesy Gerico, Inc., Gerry Baby Products

**High chairs used to be small-scaled, non-folding wooden affairs with tiny trays and hard seats. Today's gourmet baby takes her meals in state-of-the-art fashion: brightly patterned seats with safety straps, aluminum frames with wide stances, and deep, oversized trays that come off with one hand— yours, not your baby's.**

tray unless he's properly belted in with both the waist and crotch straps.

While there are no federal standards governing high chairs, the industry has developed voluntary measures that govern the safety belts, the stance, and the tray mechanisms. They require two separate steps to disengage the tray, making it nearly impossible for a toddler to accidently release the tray.

Look for a tray with a one-handed release mechanism. The logic behind such a device will become all too clear the first time you try to hold your baby and release a two-handed tray at the same time. And a nice big tray will hold more of that mashed potato and chocolate milk concoction than a smaller version, so pick one that's big and has a recessed center surrounded by a raised lip to keep all those goodies off the floor. Today's trays are usually plastic, whatever the construction of the high chair itself. Metal chairs, sometimes painted with a process called powder-coating, have the extra advantage of folding for storage, a nice plus if you don't have the room to keep a high chair open all day long.

Wooden high chairs, on the other hand, don't fold, but often blend in better with a country or colonial kitchen than metal models. They will probably hold up better over the long run than metal, a fact that is reflected in their high price tags. While some wooden high chairs continue to use wooden trays, the move is towards the larger, more versatile plastic trays.

The newcomer to the high chair market is the hook-on model that clamps on to the edge of a table, usually using the table itself instead of a separate tray for an eating surface. At first glance, you might question the design of these products, but they've become quite popular in restaurants and for traveling. The weight of the child holds the seat securely in place, although individual brands have distinctive gripping mechanisms. Some have locking devices, which are recommended here. Of course, the use of safety straps is just as important as with traditional high chairs and you also have to make sure the table itself is sturdy and stable. Some models have restrictions against use with certain tables, such as those made of glass. But because they are extremely compact, lightweight, and inexpensive, hook-ons have become a good choice for a second high chair, perhaps kept in the car trunk ready to go.

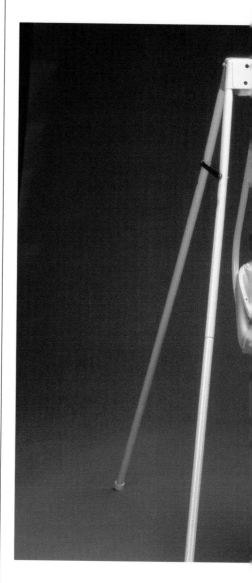

Courtesy Graco Children's Products, Inc.

**If there is one particular baby product that most people scoff at, it's the baby swing. That is, until they put their baby in one. Then, it's the greatest thing since premixed formula. Of course not every baby—or parent—needs a swing, but if your offspring just won't keep quiet, consider it.**

# Swings

A swing, in many people's minds, most perfectly typifies the baby-minder category of products: short lifespan, seemingly useless function, and no secondary purpose, but a great product for containing and entertaining your baby. A lot of parents put swings at the bottom of their should-have lists until they hear from a neighbor about the wonders they can perform. They then rush out and get one and soon they're one of the true believers, preaching the gospel of the swings.

The baby swings we're talking about here, by the way, are not to be confused with backyard jungle gym-type swings. These swings are primarily for indoor use and most feature a metal tubing, A-shaped frame with a crossbar containing the swinging mechanism. A seat hangs in the middle. Some seats are stationary, others recline, and a few deluxe models offer a swinging bassinet option. Sometimes the seat can be used independently as an infant carrier, but usually it can't be used by itself. And a few newer designs in swings feature different arcing patterns or the absence of the overhead bar, useful for easier entry and exit.

Some swings need to be wound up, others have battery-run mechanisms. Times can be set and the speed on the swing can be adjusted on deluxe models, and a few even feature built-in music boxes. The number of bells and whistles you get depends on your attraction to such things, but the battery-operated models seem to have an advantage in longer operation and quieter mechanism than the wind-ups.

As with any baby-minder, don't think you can park your little troublemaker in a swing and leave the room. But if you want to do the dishes, talk on the phone, or just relax with a cup of coffee, you'll be amazed how effective a baby swing can be for keeping your baby under control.

# Baby in the Bathroom

Next to kitchens, bathrooms represent all the best and worst in your house when it comes to your baby: The best for him because it's a great room to explore, but the worst for you because there are so many things that can go wrong in that room. That's why many parents set a hard and fast rule that the bathroom is simply off-limits to their unattended toddlers. Once he understands the word "no," you may not need special locks, but until that time—and maybe even after just as a precaution—you'll need to use a doorknob guard, a door latch, or just a key to keep the bathroom out of reach.

Regardless, there are several steps you can take in the bathroom to create a safer environment. All medicine—from aspirin to zinc oxide—should be stored in a locked cabinet and not just on a high shelf since bathroom fixtures make perfect climbing step stools for curious kids. Whenever possible, buy products with child-resistant containers. And don't forget that cleaning products represent the same kind of danger and should be kept high up and out of the way as well.

Toilets hold a special fascination for curious toddlers. They should be latched shut with any one of the number of different products on the market. Electrical appliances—

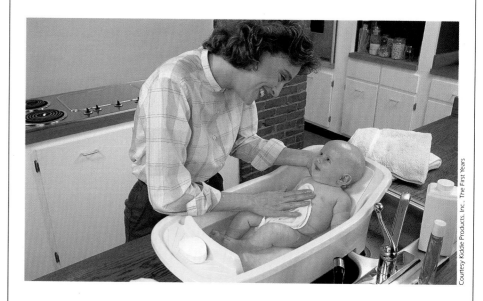

hair dryers are the obvious example, but don't forget electric toothbrushes, Water Piks, and hair curlers—should always be left unplugged and stowed away whenever possible.

Pay attention to the little things, too. If your hot water temperature is above 130°F. (54°C), lower it to between 120° and 130°F (49° and 54°C) to lessen the chance of sudden gushes of hot water causing burns. In this range, that shouldn't be a problem. Also, there are now special soft guards that fit over tub faucets and spouts to protect your baby's head when bathing. One even combines the best of both worlds with a temperature gauge to check the heat of the tap water.

You may want to have a few special toys stored in the bathroom for play only in this room. It may make the bathing process easier if your baby shows some reluctance at first to the idea of soap and water. In fact, this is a pretty good tip for all special functions, such as changing diapers or putting

on winter coats. A special music box or toy used only during these times may make things go much easier. The bath toys, by the way, can be stored in a mesh bag that hangs over the tub.

There aren't too many products specifically designed for baby that you'll be using in the bathroom, but two rate as near essentials.

## Baby Baths

Just as full-size beds are out of the question for babies, so too are full-size bathtubs. For one thing, porcelain is not the kindest of materials to wet, squirming babies. For another, the idea of you on your knees bending over the side of the tub to bathe that tiny person in what is probably too much or not enough water just doesn't make sense. The baby bath is a low-cost, ideal solution to a tricky problem. Baths come in all shapes and forms. The most popular are plastic tubs in a variety of shapes: sometimes just an oblong cavity, sometimes a contoured

Courtesy Family Life Products

The bathroom can be a fascinating place for your baby to explore—and a dangerous place for her. That's why special precautions are needed for this room. In addition to all the usual baby-proofing devices you're using elsewhere in the house, remember that the toilet, faucets, and all electrical appliances, such as hair dryers, need to be taken into consideration. Baby baths have it over adult tubs when it comes to clean-up time.

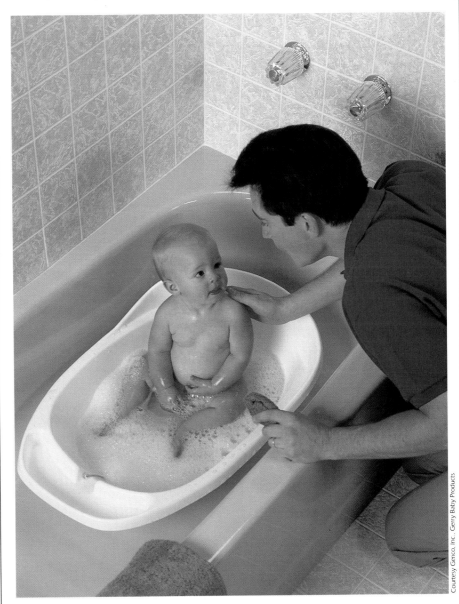

Courtesy Gerico, Inc.; Gerry Baby Products

baby-Barcalounger complete with cut-outs and indentations for soap, shampoo, and rubber duckies. On this type of tub look for a nonskid pad on the inside and a drain plug for fast clean-ups.

Another type of bath, used as an insert within another tub or as a freestanding tub in a kitchen or bathroom sink, is a foam pad that looks like a giant sponge. These are contoured for the baby's shape and provide an extra soft cushion during bathing. The

product was originally created by a California grandmother who said she dreamt it up after having a particularly anxiety-ridden bathing session while babysitting her infant granddaughter.

Baby baths come in other assorted configurations as well. One looks like an inflatable rubber tube with the center filled in to create a small well for infants. It stays in place by suction and deflates for storing. There's also the "bathinette," a freestanding

bath about the height of a changing table that can be used in the nursery itself, if a water supply is accessible.

## Toilet Trainers

You won't be using this product for some time—unfortunately for you diaper changers—but it's another piece of baby equipment you're going to need sooner or later. Trainers, also called potty chairs or seats, do exactly what you think they do and they do it in a variety of fashions. Some are freestanding, others hook onto toilets, and still others combine trainers with step stools. Almost all are made of plastic, although there are still a few older wooden designs with plastic inserts out there.

What can one say about toilet trainers? One model on the market promises to train your child in a day. Another plays, "Tinkle, tinkle, little star," whenever the proper duty is done. Some are adorned with animals' heads,

others look like the latest designer housewares products.

It's probably one of the most difficult stages a growing child—and her exasperated parent—goes through, but it always seems to bring a snicker whenever mentioned. That's why I'll avoid the urge to joke about getting to the bottom of this category or what's behind toilet trainers and just say you should examine what's on the market, talk to your pediatrician about what method is recommended, and buy a product.

# Baby All Over the House

By now, you're starting to get the hang of this baby-proofing business. So you should know what to do in the living room, den, hallways, and other assorted nooks and crannies of your household. Chances are, when your baby is in these rooms, you'll be placing him in one of the baby-minding products that work best in these areas: playpens, walkers, or swings (already covered in *Baby in the Kitchen*, page 86). But a few general suggestions are worth mentioning. Of course, watch for electrical outlets, sharp corners on tables and shelves (you can use bandages or foam rubber as temporary covers), splinters, and exposed nails and such on wooden floors and moldings. Cords from lamps, TVs, stereos, and other appliances should be taped down or enclosed in cord wrappers.

Houseplants are something some people don't consider when it comes to baby-proofing. Some, such as the common philodendron and dieffenbachia, can be quite poisonous if ingested. If you have a green thumb, it could mean moving your plants to higher ground or going without for a few years. Silk and other artificial plants can be an acceptable substitute—and think about it this way: at least you won't have to water them.

Obviously things such as

Courtesy Gerico, Inc. Gerry Baby Products

Courtesy Gerico, Inc., Gerry Baby Products

*Left:* **There are all kinds of toilet trainers on the market. This one will allow your toddler to become more independent and will get her used to climbing up on and using the big toilet.**

*Above:* **You'll be using a variety of products, most of which are optional, all around the house. However, the safety gate is an absolute necessity if your home has more than one level, and it's just about a must if you want to keep baby in or out of a certain portion of the house. Look for the newer designs and be especially careful of older, hand-me-downs when it comes to gates.**

windows without the proper guards and tabletop objects such as ashtrays and candy dishes need to be taken care of immediately. In fact, if you do smoke it's probably as good a time as ever to give another try at stopping. The idea of not having dirty ashtrays, smoldering cigarette butts, matches, and lighters around is a comforting one.

One other piece of baby-proofing equipment makes sense too, no matter what type of place you're living in.

# Gates and Enclosures

If you ever need to be reminded that small children and house pets have a lot in common, you should know that door gates for babies and door gates for pets are essentially the same product, often made by the same company but packaged differently according to its user.

Just as your cute puppy needs to be kept out of the formal living room, your cute little baby also needs to be contained in some areas. The most obvious example is staircases. In houses and apartments with more than one level, every staircase should have a gate on it. And even if you have only one floor, gates should still be used to keep wandering toddlers out of kitchens or other potentially dangerous rooms.

Gates generally are secured to the doorway or stairway by means of screw-in hardware or an expanding pressure bar

Courtesy Fisher-Price

that holds the device firmly in place. Do the installation work strictly according to instructions: good enough isn't good enough here. An aggressive baby can push in a gate that's not properly in place.

Unfortunately, some gates can be just as dangerous as a doorway with no gate at all. Up until a few years ago, many gates on the market featured an accordian-type design that created diamond and V-shaped openings when in use. These openings became entrapment areas for small heads and represented a serious hazard. You may still find

such gates in some stores and they'll certainly turn up at garage sales, flea markets, and a relative's attic. *Stay away from them.* They cannot be retrofitted for safe usage and should be avoided. In fact, I wouldn't even use them for a pet, so as far as kids go, they are out of the question.

Most gates now on the market feature rigid mesh screen panels or much smaller diamond-shaped patterns. They'll do the job just fine, and as an extra bonus, some offer a small opening door that grown-ups can open and then relock without the hassle

*Above left:* **Playpens can be a place where your baby first begins to explore her newly-expanded world. Just be sure when buying a playpen that it meets all safety standards.**

Courtesy Graco Children's Products, Inc.

*Above:* **Playpens—some people call them play yards—can be a self-contained world for your toddlin' toddler: A place for her to crawl, play, bounce around, and generally call her own. And that will suit the decor of your living room, just fine, thank you.**

of having to step over a fixed gate. Look for this feature if your gate will be in a high traffic area. Some enclosures, also called corrals, were constructed along the same lines as older gates and they too should be avoided. They provide the same kind of entrapment hazard. If you plan on using a corral-type enclosure, look for one with a different construction, such as mentioned for the gates.

## Playpens

Again, another classic baby-minder and one that you re-

ally shouldn't consider doing without is the playpen. When your baby gets a little too active for an infant seat, but isn't quite ready to roam around the house unassisted, the playpen—also called a play yard—is the perfect enclosed and protected space.

Most playpens are square and made of nylon mesh fashioned around a folding metal frame. Some models are rectangular and fit through doorways; a few come apart and can be stowed in a travel bag about the size of the sports bag you take to the gym or tennis courts. The squarish playpens also fold but use a different mechanism and don't store quite so compactly.

There are also wooden playpens still being made that resemble small cribs, but mesh designs are overwhelmingly the popular choice and probably represent a better buy.

Playpens are first and foremost used for play. Your baby can crawl around, bounce off the sides safely, pick himself up using the sides for support, learn to stand, and generally throw his toys all over the place without bothering anyone else. But you'll also find playpens a handy place for a quick nap, and when your baby's not using the pen, it can double as a storage spot for all of his toys that seem to have accumulated in the living room that day.

There are a number of safety points you should watch for if you're going with a used model or picking one up secondhand. On wooden models, watch the slat spacing, as you would on cribs, choosing one with slats no further than 2⅜ inches (approximately 6–7 centimeters) apart. Check too for the finish of the wood, lead content in the paint, and the sturdiness.

On mesh cribs, there are more things to watch out for. Most of the mesh playpens feature what are known as dropsides, which collapse for folding and to let your baby in and out. However, when the sides are down, they form a small airless pocket along their base and if an infant rolls over into this pocket, he can suffocate. It's a design element common to almost all dropside playpens and if you choose to use this convenient type of model, you can't ever let the child use the product with the dropside down.

All newer dropside playpens carry a warning label, but older models may not. Label or not, the use pattern is the same. *Keep the dropside up.* That goes for times when your baby is outside the playpen and could crawl back into it from the outside.

On used or older playpens, also check for tears or rips in the vinyl or fabric-covered rails and pads. Tiny pieces can be bitten off by teething toddlers and cause him to choke. Also look for loose threads, missing staples (that's how some vinyl is attached to the rigid floor board), and mesh with large holes or sections missing. All can cause problems. The mesh itself should have holes no larger than about a quarter

of an inch (one half centimeter) wide. Hardware and locking mechanisms should be inspected for sharp edges and ease of operation.

Be careful of toys placed in playpens. Big ones can be used as steps to climb over the sides and should be removed. Small ones shouldn't be strung across the top of the playpen because of strangulation hazards. If you do want to tie a toy, use a string twelve inches (thirty centimeters) or less in length and secure it to the side of the playpen. In general follow the same toy rules you do for your baby's crib.

Choose a playpen design according to your lifestyle. You may get a few stares from people in the store—and glares from the salespeople—but ask to see a demonstration of how the playpen folds. If you're a Have-Baby-Will-Travel-type family you'll be performing that ritual an awful lot over the next year or two, so see how easy it really is.

Finally, the inside advice on playpens is that if you're going to use one, start early. A street-smart six-month-old is going to think he's being caged in, rather than being given his own little play world, if you wait until that age. A few naps or visits to this place before your child is really ready for it can leave the lasting impression that it's a playpen and not just *the* pen.

## Walkers

One more baby-minder you may not mind yourself is the

*Above:* **Walkers should perhaps more accurately be called almost-walkers, because that's when baby uses them. A wide stance is a must when it comes to these products, and you should check for locking mechanisms and exposed hardware. Some new designs now lock when going over uneven surfaces such as stairs—a nice safety feature.**

Courtesy Cosco, Inc.

walker, which you've probably gathered is a somewhat different product than your arthritic aunt uses to help get her around. But interestingly enough, both products perform essentially the same task: to help those whose walking and stability is impaired or not yet quite what it should be.

Baby walkers allow a trying-to-walk baby to move about, courtesy of a set of wheels beneath what sometimes resembles a bumper car made of plastic. Other walkers enlist an exposed X-shaped frame, but all essentially have a cloth or fabric-covered suspended seat where your baby sits and semi-controls his movements. Some walkers look like little cars, others have a suspended string of toys and most have a tray, sometimes sporting several small, built-in play functions. There is no steering or any controls, per se, but babies seem to love walkers.

Whether you like them is another story. They do allow you to let your baby scoot about the house or gated-in area without constant supervision. But they also allow your baby to bump into things faster and more haphazardly than if he was crawling. He's also at a different height now, which makes a whole other round of baby-proofing and house cleaning necessary.

And walkers do have design elements that can present problems. They tend to tip more easily than other juvenile products especially when going over rugs or as your baby leans over to grab some-thing. So look for a walker with as wide a base as possible. Watch walker hardware, too, as it tends to be closer to baby's reach than in some other products. All folding mechanisms and metal parts should be smooth, have covers where needed, especially over coil springs, and have sturdy locking devices.

And of course, since walkers are on wheels, the use of gates becomes all the more necessary around stairs and even single steps near front doors or leading into a step-down living room, for instance. Just coming onto the market are walkers with automatic locks that freeze when going off an edge, but as with any juvenile product, a walker is only as safe as the parent who's keeping an eye out.

It can't be said often enough that baby-minders are not baby sitters. A walker can provide some peace of mind for you and some real play value for your baby, but it is a product that most certainly requires careful shopping, solid planning, and close attention.

# Baby Outside the House

No matter how safe and cozy an environment you've created for your baby in your house, sooner or later you're going to take her out into the real world. In the old days, many babies stayed indoors for most of the first year of their lives. Now, between doctor's appointments, shopping trips, day trips, and plain old vacations, babies have become as mobile as the rest of the family. And today's well-traveled baby has a host of products available for her use to make those trips not only safer, but also more enjoyable for both of you. In fact, babies on the go have become such a common sight that the creation of a warning sign for cars a few years back, reading "Baby On Board," created a national phenomenon.

Traveling with your baby doesn't have to be an ordeal and shouldn't be considered a big production. Once you have a baby, you don't want to become a shut-in. All you need is the right equipment, and a little common sense.

Obviously, the first thing you want is to make certain that your baby is dressed correctly for the weather. Too many times too bulky a snowsuit or too light a top can make for a cranky and uncomfortable baby. Headgear re-

mains probably the single most overlooked item for your baby, whatever the temperature conditions outside.

Another practical tip is to prepare and always have ready a baby travel bag. It can be an extra diaper bag, a knapsack, or any similarly sized piece of luggage you won't be needing on a regular basis. Start off your travel checklist with enough diapers—disposable or cloth, depending on what you use—to last for a full day's outing.

Next, put in a small fold-up or roll-up changing pad and some small packages of the pre-moistened towelettes, cream, and the various protective ointments you use for changing. You can include a can of spray disinfectant for the area where you'll be changing your baby. Next, stick in a few plastic bags with ties for used diapers. Finish off your bag with an extra change of clothing, a pacifier, and a small toy or two.

By having this bag ready to go all the time—and checking it every once in a while to replenish and replace supplies—impromptu or unexpected trips needn't be an ordeal. You'll be more likely to take spur-of-the-moment rides or walks and that's going to make your baby more comfortable, which means a happier baby and a happier you.

But the key to any trip outside the house is having the right equipment.

## Car Seats

You wouldn't let your baby sleep on a chair in her nursery, would you? It's the same thing as letting her ride in an automobile unrestrained. As important as a crib is to your baby's room, that's how essential a car seat is to your baby's car ride.

It's taken a long time for the American public to get used to the idea of restraining devices—for both babies and adults—when riding in a car,

Courtesy Gerico, Inc. Gerry Baby Products

*Right:* **There's no if, ands, or buts about infant automobile restraining devices (car seats). They are an absolute necessity for any auto trip, be it around the corner or across the country. And they're also the law, in all fifty states and the District of Columbia.**

*Left:* **For fast getaways, always have a daytripping bag packed and ready to go. An extra diaper bag or small piece of luggage kept handy can do wonders for impromptu adventures.**

Courtesy Cosco, Inc.

but today no one can dispute it's the safest way to travel. Parents used to think they were doing their baby a favor by holding her on their laps when traveling, but unfortunately, this was the worst thing that could be done.

An unrestrained baby during a panic stop or a crash will become a hurtling missile, thrown about the interior of the car, crashing through the windshield, or being crushed by a bigger person. If you were brought up not wearing seat belts, don't make your baby pay for your hard-to-

break bad habits. Get him in a car seat, from his very first ride home from the hospital.

Even in normal driving situations, car seats are a nice thing to have around. They keep toddlers from jumping around the car, touching all the knobs on the dashboard, playing with the windows, and generally annoying and distracting everyone else in the vehicle. If your child knows that being in her car seat is the only way she's going to ride in a car—and she sees you buckle up your safety belt—pretty soon she's going

to accept it as just another rule of the game like sleeping in her crib and being fed in her high chair.

If you need any more convincing about the importance of using children's car seats, consider that you'll now be breaking the law in all 50 states if your child isn't properly restrained. Every state, plus the District of Columbia, now has a law on the books requiring that young children be correctly restrained when traveling. Penalties go as high as $300 fines and points on your driver's license, but even if your chances of being caught are slim, you should put your baby in a car seat simply because it's the right—and safe—thing to do.

Car seats come in a variety of shapes and configurations. Most feature a hard plastic shell usually supported by a frame made of metal tubing. Some have bars or shields that swing down over and rest in front of the child and contain restraining straps while other models have only the straps; sometimes three, sometimes five, all of which interlock in a central buckle.

Most models on the market today come in darker colors such as blacks, greys, blues, and browns to match car interiors. Most will have vinyl pads, but some will have cloth covers, and there's even a leather-covered model available now. You can also purchase removable and replaceable covers.

All children's car seats on the market are tested by the federal government in simulated crash sequences, a process called dynamic testing. They must meet criteria set forth in a regulation called Federal Motor Vehicle Safety Standard No. 213. If you're going with a used car seat or dragging an old model down from the attic and it doesn't say it complies with standard No. 213 (which went into effect in 1978), don't use it. Old car seats can't be updated to meet the standard and under no circumstances should they be used in an automobile.

You'll have several choices

when it comes to buying a car seat or car seats, depending on what you select. Infant car seats—and again, don't confuse car seats with infant carrier seats used for feeding and napping but absolutely *not* safe as car restraint devices—look like little buckets and provide a shell-like seat for travel. You can use these infant seats for the first nine to ten months of your baby's traveling days, or until she's about seventeen to twenty pounds, depending on the exact model.

If it's an infant-only model, you then must retire that car seat and move up to a child or toddler-sized model. There are also convertible car seats that can be used by both size ranges, by flipping them around 180° for each use. These bigger and older car seats can be used up until the time your child is about four years old, or forty pounds.

Whether you buy a convertible model or separate infant and toddler seats is largely dependent on your budget. Infant models, because they are designed for just one purpose, tend to provide a slightly better fit for small babies than convertible seats. But buying one seat—and some of them get pretty expensive in the $50 to $80 range—is a nice cost savings. The final decider may be whether you have more than one very young child. If you need two car seats, separate models may make sense. Otherwise, the convertible will probably do just fine.

A third, newer, car seat is the toddler booster seat,

which raises an older child—age four to about seven—up to window-viewing height and provides for proper restraint, yet gives the upper body more freedom of movement. As these are specifically designed for automobile use, don't confuse them with indoor booster seats sometimes used to raise small children up at the dinner table. They won't do the job in case there's trouble.

An improperly installed car seat—of whatever size—won't do the job either. This is another product where almost right isn't good enough. Car seats are held in place by one

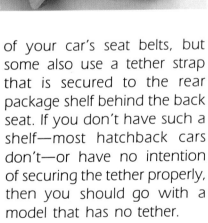

Courtesy Fisher-Price

*Left:* **Just having a car seat isn't enough. It has to be properly installed—and then your baby has to be properly installed into it, or the whole thing is useless. Car seats come in three basic varieties: infant-only models for your baby's first nine to ten months; convertible models for use until your baby reaches about 40 pounds; and toddler booster seats, through about age seven. And yes, the middle of the back seat is the best location for any car seat.**

of your car's seat belts, but some also use a tether strap that is secured to the rear package shelf behind the back seat. If you don't have such a shelf—most hatchback cars don't—or have no intention of securing the tether properly, then you should go with a model that has no tether.

Infant, toddler, and booster seats should all be installed in the back seat and in the middle of the back seat if at all possible. Yes, your tendency is to have your baby up front with you, but the back seat is the safest place in the car and that's where you want your baby.

If your car seat isn't installed correctly, it's almost as bad as not having a car seat at all. That's how important it is. So follow the instructions. Equally as critical is that your baby be properly installed as well. A good idea before you buy anything is to see how easy it is to buckle your baby into the device. Different models have different configurations of straps and buckles and you should see which is the most comfortable set-up for you. Use a doll in the store for practice and see how smoothly it goes. Obviously, your technique will get better as you go along, but it's impossible the

first time, it's only going to get tolerable later on and that's not good enough.

If you're on a fixed budget, many local childbirth groups and hospitals will rent or loan you a car seat for a small fee. However you get one, *make sure you have a car seat—a current model, correctly installed, with all belts in the right places.* Along with a crib, it's the most important single purchase you'll make.

By the way, if your family does a lot of airplane traveling, you should know that many children's car seats have also been certified by the Federal Aviation Administration for use in commercial airlines. Look for the FAA approval symbol on packaging if that's a consideration for you.

## Strollers and Carriages

Big, handsome, but incredibly cumbersome and heavy, carriages used to be the only way to wheel your baby around town. But compact cars, condos, and shopping malls have changed all of that, and while some might miss the romance and pageantry of the formal baby perambulator, today's wheeled products are the state of the art.

Many strollers now on the market are almost mini-carriages in that they feature a full-recline position just as carriages offer. But then they can revert to the stroller mode with the flick of the handle and a few latches. They are remarkable devices and in fact, one could probably never figure out how to use all of the features on some of today's products.

Other strollers are strictly strollers and they range from the most rudimentary designs—essentially a sling seat in a lightweight folding aluminum frame—all the way up to deluxe versions with swivel wheels, contoured seats, armrests, and plush interiors. Some even have sunroofs so you can peek in through the canopy and see how your little passenger is enjoying the ride.

Whatever design you choose—and some parents are buying two strollers: a lightweight model to keep in the car trunk for quick trips and a more full-featured version for longer strolls—there are certain things to watch for. As with any baby product on wheels, you'll want a wide stance for stability. Locking mechanisms and other hardware should be checked for finish, ease of operation, and

*Right:* **For the free-wheelin' baby, today's modern stroller is the way to go. Many have full-reclining modes for naptime but convert easily into upright positions. And they fold for easy storage in all but the smallest car trunks.**

durability. See how strong the brakes are and how easy they are to release. The same goes for reclining devices and canopies: They need to stay in place tightly once you've chosen a position. And of course, strollers are another product that have safety straps to hold your baby securely in place.

Check the fabric. Some strollers are covered in vinyl, easy to clean but sticky and uncomfortable in the heat, and cold and uncomfortable when the temperature drops. More often you'll find cloth seat covers, most of which are removable for washing. You can also purchase separate covers that will brighten up a stroller seat that may have seen better days.

Strollers are built to put up with a lot of use and abuse, but they're not indestructible. Although many people load them down with packages after a day at the mall or supermarket, it must be remembered they are designed for human cargo first and fore-

most. If you need something to hold boxes and bags, get a shopping cart. Save your stroller for your baby.

Carriages still do exist and if you must have one—or more likely want to use a family heirloom or hand-me-down—you'll know they are comfortable, weather-protective, and sturdy. They are also big, none too compact even if they do partially fold, and quite heavy to lug up and down steps and in and out of cars. If you're using an older model, check for working brakes and secure safety straps. If you're buying a new carriage, you can follow the same general rules as for purchasing a stroller.

With the exception of cribs, no other product for your baby comes in as many different configurations and price ranges. You can pay nineteen dollars, on sale, for the most basic stroller, or more than three hundred dollars for a model with every conceivable (and some almost inconceivable) features. Carriages go even higher. Again, decide on your lifestyle, how often you'll be using it, whether it has to last for more than one child, and just generally how hard you are on moving parts. But don't underbuy a stroller, because in strollers, more than most baby products, you get what you pay for.

## Backpack Carriers

One last outdoor travel product is a more recent invention but has attracted a number of devotees over the past several

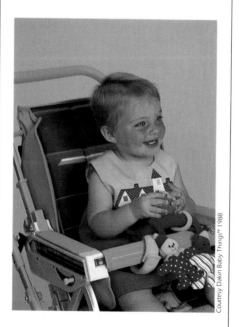

Courtesy Dakin Baby Things™ 1988

decades. Born out of the backpacking and hiking industry, the baby backpack—with or without aluminum frame—has become a popular choice for transporting your baby while keeping your hands free. And these carriers are not just being used outdoors anymore, either.

Backpack carriers—and that's a slight misnomer because some packs aren't worn on the back—come in two general varieties. The first design has a canvas carrier mounted on a lightweight aluminum frame, much like a hiking backpack. The frame is placed on your back, with the weight evenly distributed across your shoulders. Some of these products can also stand by themselves, giving them a second function in a pinch. Other carriers use fabric straps, in a variety of configurations, instead of a hard frame. These packs can be worn on the back, but some can also be worn on your chest and a few can be slung on your side. Deluxe models allow for multiple positions. These carriers are available in cloth, nylon, denim, corduroy, and even seersucker.

There are also some carriers meant to be worn exclusively on your chest. These tend to be of soft, non-framed construction, again made of fabric, usually cotton or nylon. The baby is supported in a pouch-type compartment, with the weight evenly distributed across your shoulders. This type of carrier also promotes a greater bonding be-

Courtesy Gerico, Inc. Gerry Baby Products

*Left:* **While baby backpack carriers are normally kept for outdoor use, they also can be used inside, allowing your baby to tag along while you go about your daily chores. Some carriers are worn on the front or the side and some convert depending on baby's age.**

tween parent and baby. On some carriers, the baby faces inward—good for a fast and secure nap—while on others, she gazes the same way you do, which makes for great sightseeing. When deciding which type of carrier you want, consider the position that will be most comfortable for you: your baby on your back or on your chest.

On both types of carriers, the first criterion is comfort: both yours and your baby's. Make sure your baby has plenty of head and body support and that openings for legs and arms are the right size. Then see how it feels on you, preferably with your baby in it. Look for cushioned straps, heavy-duty snaps, and quality sewing. Again, use a doll— the heavier the better—if your own living doll isn't available. Try to test it out as long as possible to see how it feels after a prolonged period of use. It should be easy to put on and take off and you shouldn't need assistance from three passing strangers to put your baby in it.

A backpack carrier certainly doesn't rate as a necessity. Many parents get along just fine without one. But if you have an outdoor lifestyle that involves a lot of walking—and you don't want to give that up just because you've had a baby—back carriers are a much better choice than strollers. They won't replace a stroller, but they make a nice addition.

Some people even use their back carriers indoors. If you've got a million things to do around the house, but want to keep baby close-by, strap on a carrier, load up your passenger, and get to work. Your baby may love the activity and the chance to be near you. Your hands will be free and you won't have to keep running back to the playpen to check how things are going.

Back carriers are one of those little products that you don't have to have, but they can make this whole baby thing a little easier and more enjoyable. Maybe you could drop a few hints around baby shower time.

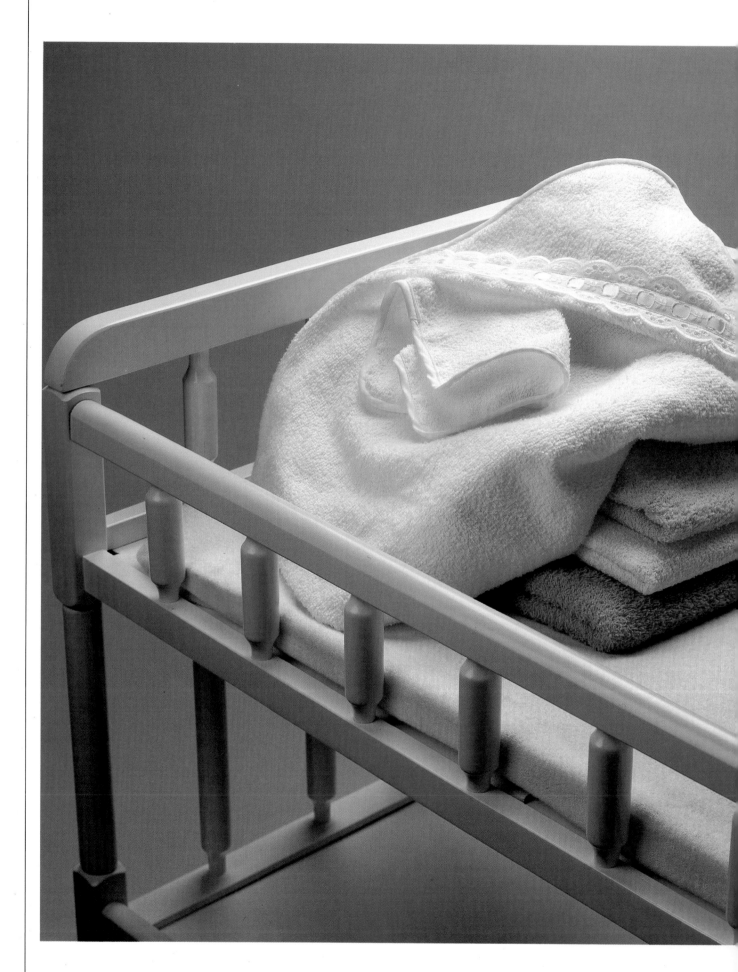

CHAPTER 6

# The Who, What, & Where of Baby Rooms

Y ou are just about ready to receive your diploma in Baby Rooms 101. You've learned how to build, buy, and borrow. You've discovered what products are necessary and which ones are frivolous luxuries. You've dealt with the age-old battle of primary colors versus soft pastels. You've seen how batteries have changed the face of bringing up baby. And you've found how to deal with your baby outside of the nursery.

This final chapter is a quick review of the safety requirements governing all the key products. We've also included a suggested list of products you'll need to get started with this baby business. There are also some names and addresses of agencies and organizations you may want to contact along the way. Take these lists with you when you go shopping or use them as checklists when you get back home.

# What You Need to Know

The products you'll be using for your baby are covered by a myriad of assorted rules, regulations, and standards. Some are federally mandated, but not all come from the same federal agencies. Others are set by individual states. Several standards are voluntary, created by the juvenile products industry with government approval. And some products on the market aren't covered by any rules at all.

Sorting it out can be a real chore, so following is a list of basic products, what if any regulations cover them, and a brief rundown of safety measures to look for.

A few ground rules first. If a product has a mandatory federal safety standard covering it, the government agency involved is usually the Consumer Product Safety Commission. Created in the early 1970s, the CPSC is an independent regulatory body under the executive wing of the federal government. Besides juvenile products and toys, it covers a wide variety of consumer products from lawn mowers to furniture.

The one exception at the federal level involves car seats, which are regulated by the National Highway Traffic Safety Administration, a division of the Department of Transportation. The reasoning behind this is that car seats are a motor vehicle-related product and should be regulated accordingly. If you call the CPSC and ask them about car seats, they will refer you to the NHTSA. It pays to know your alphabet.

Car seats are also the one product regulated by individual states, although in this respect it's a matter of usage rather than construction or design. Each state has a rule on the books requiring car seat use up to various ages, in some cases ranging up through age eleven. Your state government has to be consulted for the latest local requirements.

You'll also come across voluntary safety standards. These have been developed by the manufacturers of the products themselves, using outside standards-writing organizations. The federal government, through the CPSC, approves the process, although the commission never actually endorses a specific measure. The whole process may sound a little self-serving, but it

Courtesy Lillian Vernon Corp

works and has brought safer products to the marketplace faster and less expensively than if the mandatory federal regulation route had been followed.

The products covered by voluntary measures are tested and certified by the trade association of manufacturers, the Juvenile Products Manufacturers Association. Products that pass these tests will carry a JPMA Certification Seal on both their packaging and product literature. It's a good symbol to watch for. A trade group of companies that makes toys, the Toy Manufacturers of America, also is involved in creating voluntary safety standards, although they have no seal indicating their approval.

As for the products not covered under any regulations, some may fall under general standards for small parts or paint content, for instance. And some just don't seem to have any definable qualities that can be measured and

Other than the most basic basics—cribs and car seats—no one can say what you absolutely *must* have. Whatever you select, however, should meet the basic criteria described in this chapter.

tested. So, on the following list, note some good old commonsense rules to remember when shopping for these items.

## Backpack Carriers

*Standard: none*
*Safety Features: Look for sturdy construction, smoothly finished frames, correctly sized leg and arm openings, and good head and body support for your baby.*
*Buying Tips: Look for padded straps and ease of putting on pack with your baby.*

## Bassinets and Cradles

*Standard: none*
*Safety Features: Look for a wide base for stability and sturdy locking mechanism.*
*Buying Tips: Product has very short lifespan, so don't overbuy quality you'll never need or use.*

## Baths

*Standard: none*
*Safety Features: Look for non-skid coating on bottom and inside of tub area.*
*Buying Tips: Some baths are contoured to fit your baby's shape and many have plugs, making draining easier.*

## Bedding

*Standard: none*
*Safety Features: Watch for decorative or functional ribbons or strings more than 12 inches (30 centimeters) long which could cause strangulation.*
*Buying Tips: Many crib ensembles come with as many as twenty coordinating accessory pieces.*

## Car Seats

*Standard: Mandatory Federal NHTSA #213*
*Safety Features: All products on market meet standard, but look for one with easy installation, simple seat belt latching mechanism, and smoothly finished metal frame. Almost every state and the District of Columbia require that children ride in car seats up through at least age four (Alabama and Wyoming up to age three and Mississippi up to age two are the exceptions).*
*Buying Tips: A convertible seat may be more economical than separate infant and toddler car seats. Also look for models with reclining features and removable fabric for cleaning.*

## Carrier Seats

*Standard: none*
*Safety Features: Look for wide, sturdy base for stability, nonskid bottom, and easy-to-use crotch strap.*
*Buying Tips: Some carrier seats have small storage compartments, which can be handy, and some have removable fabric for cleaning.*

## Changing Tables

*Standard: none*
*Safety Features: Look for safety straps and closed storage area near changing surface.*
*Buying Tips: Some changing tables convert to a second use, such as a desk or bookcase, which gives the product a longer lifespan.*

## Cribs

*Standard: Mandatory Federal CPSC Rules*
*Safety Features: All products on market meet standard. If using an older crib manufactured before 1974, slats must be spaced no further than 2 3/8 inches (6–7 centimeters) apart and the mattress should fit snugly into frame with less than two inches (5 centimeters) width between edge and crib side. Also check mattress support, lead content in paint, and dual-action dropside mechanism. There should be no cut-outs in head and footboard to allow head entrapment and corner posts shouldn't be more than 5/8 of an inch (approximately 1 cen-*

timeter) higher than the crib side to prevent entanglement.
*Buying Tips: Some cribs convert to youth beds, but are expensive. Many cribs have matching case pieces—dressers and chests—available, but some, such as brass models, usually don't.*

## Dressers and Chests

*Standard: none*
*Safety Features: Make sure used furniture has not been painted with lead-based paint, which must be removed. Watch for baby-level sharp corners and edges.*
*Buying Tips: Look for fine furniture features such as dovetail joints and dust liners between drawers.*

## Gates and Enclosures

*Standard: JPMA Voluntary Measure*
*Safety Features: Do not use old-style products with large diamond and V-shaped areas that can entrap small heads. Look for newer models with smaller openings and sturdy mounting mechanisms.*
*Buying Tips: Some gates have hardware that won't mar walls and some feature pass-through doors for adults.*

## High Chairs

*Standard: JPMA Voluntary Measure*
*Safety Features: Look for wide stance for stability, dependable and easy-to-use restraining straps, no sharp edges,*

and dual-action tray. If high chair folds, it should have a sturdy locking mechanism.
*Buying Tips: Wide, deep trays that can be removed with one hand are preferable. A slim folding position makes for easier storage.*

## Pacifiers, Rattles and Teethers

*Standard: CPSC Mandatory Measure*
*Safety Features: None of these products should have ribbons, yarns, or strings big enough to go around your baby's head. Pacifier shields should be big enough not to fit in your baby's mouth. Rattles and teethers should be at least two inches (five centimeters) inches in diameter to prevent choking. There should be no small parts on any of these products that can be removed and swallowed.*
*Buying Tips: Silicone pacifiers look fresher after repeated use than latex pacifiers.*

## Playpens

*Standard: JPMA Voluntary Measure*
*Safety Features: Dropside mesh playpens must not be used with sides down, creating a suffocation hazard. Mesh weave should be small—less than quarter-inch (half-centimeter) openings—and there should be no loose mesh, torn vinyl, or exposed sharp hardware.*
*Buying Tips: Some playpens fit through doorway openings,*

Courtesy Lillian Vernon Corp

**There are literally thousands of toys available for your baby. Make sure whatever you select meets basic requirements for small parts that can be pulled off and swallowed.**

important if you move them from room to room, and some pack up in duffle-bag-style cases, important if you travel a lot with your playpen.

## Strollers and Carriages

*Standard: JPMA Voluntary Measure*
*Safety Features: Look for wide, stable base, secure restraining strap, strong brakes, and no sharp edges on exposed hardware.*
*Buying Tips: Many full-feature strollers convert to a carriage mode, but tend to be bulkier than lighter models that only have a stroller function. Look for a strong back support, and adjustable height handle if you're especially tall.*

## Swings

*Standard: none*
*Safety Features: Look for wide base for stability, no sharp surfaces on exposed hardware, and secure restraining strap.*

*Buying Tips: Battery-operated models are quieter and usually will run longer at one time than hand-operated crank swings. Some models have adjustable speed and even music boxes.*

## Toilet Trainers

*Standard: none*
*Safety Features: If the model fits into an adult fixture, look for a secure fit. If the product is made of wood, look for a smooth finish, free of splinters.*
*Buying Tips: Some toilet trainers can be used both freestanding and in conjunction with adult fixtures and some double as step stools. Look for a model with easy cleaning design.*

## Toy Chests

*Standard: TMA Voluntary Measure*
*Safety Features: Most important is a spring-loaded lid support that holds the lid in any position, preventing the lid*

from slamming down. Also look for ventilation holes or spaces, and make sure there are no latches to lock the chest when it is closed.
*Buying Tips: An open-style toy chest might encourage better clean-ups. Also consider bins inside the chest to organize toys and make them more accessible.*

## Walkers

*Standard: CPSC Federal Mandatory Measure*
*Safety Features: Products must have frame design that won't collapse or cause entrapment problems. In addition, look for a wide stance, mechanisms that are covered or out of reach, and properly sized leg openings.*
*Buying Tips: Some walkers have big trays for play and occasional feeding uses, and some have a few built-in toys. Locking mechanisms, activated when going over uneven surfaces, are also turning up on some models now.*

Courtesy Motif Designs/Wallpaper & Fabric by Marimekko Little People

# Where's My List of What I Really Need?

Some new parents will buy a crib, a car seat, and a high chair and say their job is finished. Others will head for the juvenile furniture aisle of Toys 'R' Us and tell the sales clerk they'll take one of everything. You'll probably fall somewhere in the middle.

The following is a list of basic furniture, furnishings, and accessories you'll most likely need for your new baby and your new baby's room. Some items, such as feeding accessories and baby hygiene products, haven't been discussed in this book, but since they're pretty fundamental items, you should get the hang of them pretty quickly. Also included is a list of clothing needs that will get you through the first few months.

In addition, there is a list of

**If you're not sure if you *really* need a product, try going without it and see what happens. You'll either be surprised by how badly you need it, or reassured you made the right decision in holding off.**

some optional equipment and products you may want to have for your baby. You may think some of them frivolous and some absolute necessities. That's why your baby's room is going to be different from your neighbor's.

Finally, there are probably dozens—make that hundreds—of other products out there that you're going to run into. They're not on any list, they're not covered in any chapter in this book—in fact, some of them probably weren't even invented when this book was being written. You're going to simply love some of them—and get taken to the cleaners on some others. Let the buyer beware.

## Furniture and Furnishings

Bath
Car seat
Carrier seat
Changing table/dresser
Crib

High Chair
Mattress
Monitor
Playpen
Safety latches, covers, and accessories, as needed
Stroller
*Optional:*
Backpack carrier
Birth announcements
Carriage
Chest of drawers
Coordinated nursery accessories
Cradle or bassinet
Crib mobile
Diaper bag
Diaper pail
Gates
Laundry hamper
Nursery lamp
Portable crib
Scale
Storage units
Swing
Table and chair set
Toilet trainer
Toy box
Vaporizer
Walker

## Bedding and Bathing

Assorted toiletries, including soap, powder, moist towelettes, petroleum jelly, and ointments
Baby scissors
Baby shampoo
Baby thermometer (rectal)
Bedding ensembles
Brush and comb set
Crib blankets, 2–3
Crib bumper
Crib comforter
Crib sheets, 4–6
Quilted crib pads, 2
Towels, hand and bath, 4
Washcloths

*Optional:*
Additional sheets and bedding
Waterproof pads or sheets

## Feeding Equipment

Bibs, 4
Bottle and nipple brush
Bottle feeding: 8 bottles, sterilizer kit, utensils
Breast feeding: 2–4 bottles, nipple shields, nursing pads, breast cream, and breast pump
Disposable bottles
Feeding dish or dishes, utensils

## Clothing and Apparel

Booties or socks
Cloth diapers: 3–4 dozen if home washed; 80–100 a week if you use a service
Cold weather outerwear as needed
Cotton shirts, 6
Disposable diaper liners
Disposable diapers: 10–12 per day
Gowns, 3
Hat or bonnet
Kimonos, 3
Receiving blankets, 3–5
Sacque sets, 3
Safety pins as needed
Shoes
Stretch suits, 3
Sweater set

# Organizations That Can Help

There are a number of agencies, groups, and organizations that can provide further information on specific subjects or can be consulted when a problem comes up. Each one can help make your baby's room a little better, a little brighter, and a little safer.

*American Academy of Pediatrics*
Committee on Accident and Poison Prevention
141 Northwest Point Road
P.O. Box 927
Elk Grove Village, IL 60007
General information on child care and products

*Chemical Specialties Manufacturers Association*
1001 Connecticut Avenue, Suite 1120, N.W.
Washington, D.C. 20036
Provides a paid (75¢ plus 45¢ postage) information booklet on "Your Child and Household Safety."

*Juvenile Products Manufacturers Association*
66 East Main St.
Moorestown, NJ 08057

Trade group of baby products manufacturers has several brochures available on selecting safe products.

*National Safety Council*
Home Safety Department
P.O. Box 11933
Chicago, IL 60611
Has general information about making households safer.

*National Passenger Safety Association*
P.O. Box 65616
Washington, D.C. 20035
Publishes a free annual car seat shopping guide.

*Toy Manufacturers of America*
200 Fifth Avenue
New York, NY 10010
Trade group of toy manufacturers has general information on selecting safe products for infants and children.

*U.S. Consumer Product Safety Commission*
Washington, D.C. 20207
Federal agency that regulates many baby products and maintains a hotline to receive product information, order educational literature, and report hazards and product defects.

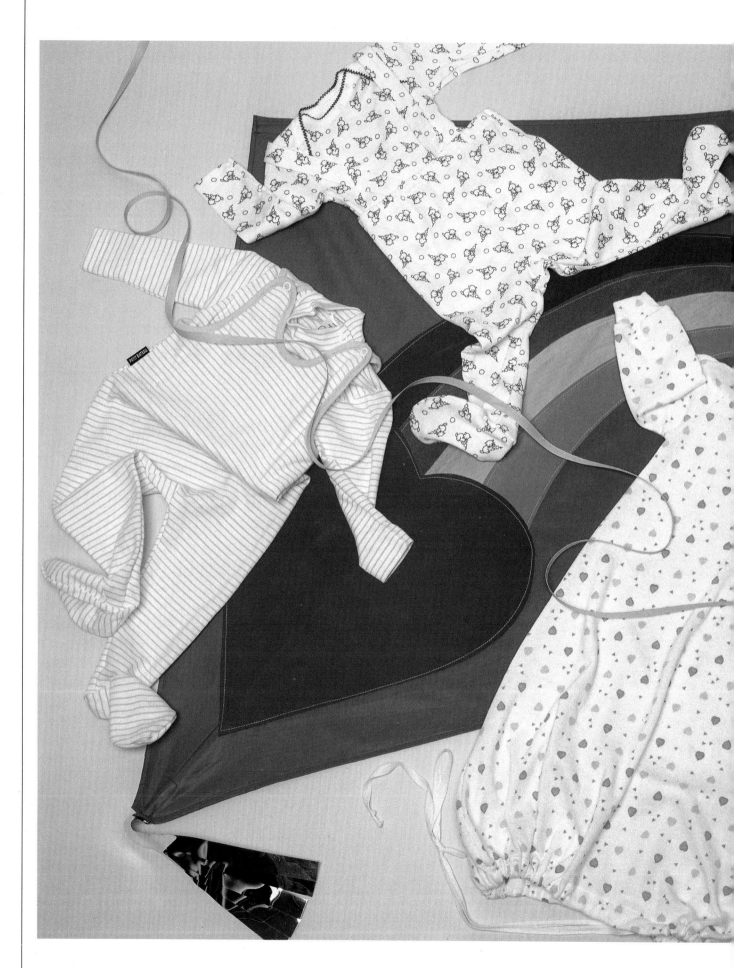

114

Photo by Robert Gray

# Sources and Index

# Sources

**Bright Ideas**
51 Meade Avenue
Box 41062
Pittsburgh, PA 15202

**Century Products**
Gerber Furniture Group Inc.
9600 Valley View Road
Macedonia, OH 44056

**Child Safety Products**
P.O. Box 668
Walla Walla, WA 99362

**Child Craft**
P.O. Box 444
Salem, IN 47167

**Clairson International**
720 South West 17th Street
Ocala, FL 32674

**Cosco, Inc.**
Juvenile Products Group
2525 State Street
Columbus, IN 47201

**Family Life Products**
Box K
Dennis, MA 02638

**Fisher-Price**
636 Girard Avenue
East Aurora, NY 14052

**Gerico, Inc.**
Snugli Inc.
Gerry Baby Products
12520 Grant Drive
P.O. Box 33755
Denver, CO 80233

**Graco Children's
Products, Inc.**
Route 23 Box 300
Elverson, PA 19520

**Hasbro, Inc.**
1027 Newport Avenue
P.O. Box 1059
Pawtucket, RI 02862

**Judi's**
7855 East Evans
Scottsdale, AZ 85260

**Kiddie Products, Inc.**
The First Years
One Kiddie Drive
Avon, MA 02322

**Lambs & Ivy**
8944 Lindblade Street
Culver City, CA 90230

**Lillian Vernon**
510 South Fulton Avenue
Mount Vernon, NY 10550

**The Little Tikes Co.**
2180 Barlow Road
Hudson, OH 44236

**Lullabye Garden**
3819 Gardenia
Long Beach, CA 90807

**Mattel Toys**
5150 Rosencrans Avenue
Hawthorne, CA 90250

**Merryland By Marilyn**
7406 Valjean Avenue
Van Nuys, CA 91406

**Motif Designs**
20 Jones Street
New Rochelle, NY 10801

**Nasta Industries**
200 Fifth Avenue
New York, NY 10010

**The Newborne Co.**
River Road
Worthington, MA 01098

**Noel-Joanna, Inc.**
One Mason
Irvine, CA 92714

**Pat Higdon Industries**
P.O. Drawer 980
Quincy, FL 32351

**Petco Prints**
12 Linscott Road
Woburn, MA 01801

**Playskool Baby, Inc.**
108 Fairway Court
Northvale, NJ 07647

**Premarq, Inc.**
P.O. Box 840
Astoria, OR 97103

**Priss Prints**
3002 Jeremes Landing
Garland, TX 75043

**Puck Children's Furniture**
3620 North West 59th Street
Miami, FL 33142

**Strolee of California**
19067 Reyes
Rancho Dominguez, CA
90221

**Summer Infant
Products Inc.**
711 Branch Avenue
Providence, RI 02904

**Taylor Made Creations**
4240 Old Farm Road
Oklahoma City, OK 73120

**Turn on Toys**
2300 Wisconsin Ave. N.W.
Washington, DC 20007

**Welsh Company**
1535 South Eighth Street
St. Louis, MO 63104

# Index